# PROTE
# ANI
# APPEALS

The rain it raineth on the just
And also on the unjust fella
But chiefly on the just because
The unjust steals the just's umbrella

*Lord Bowen*

# PROTESTS AND APPEALS

## A Competitor's Guide

Bryan Willis

*fernhurst*
BOOKS

First published by Fernhurst Books, Duke's Path, High Street, Arundel,
West Sussex, BN18 9AJ, UK

Printed and bound in Great Britain

British Library Cataloguing in Publication Data:
A catalogue record for this book is available from the British Library.

ISBN 1 - 898660 -17 - 4

Acknowledgments

The publishers would like to thank Goran Petersson and
Liv Sherwood for their very helpful comments on the manuscript.

Photographic credits
All photos courtesy of KOS except
p12-13: C. Hufstader, courtesy of Glenn Bourke
p16, 23 & 29: Christel Clear
p39: The Laser Centre
p55 and cover: Peter Bentley

Also by Bryan Willis
The Rules in Practice

DTP by Creative Byte, Bournemouth
Cover design by Simon Balley
Printed and bound by Ebenezer Baylis & Son, Worcester
Text set in 9pt Rockwell

# Contents

# ACKNOWLEDGMENTS

I am indebted to the many international Judges and Umpires with whom I have worked since 1981 when the International Judges Scheme started. Many have shared countless hours in hearings and afterwards addressing interesting situations and discussing possible rule changes in the hope of making the game of yacht racing more enjoyable. Some have walked with me down the difficult and sometimes perilous road investigating cheating and imposing heavy penalties on that tiny minority who try to win unfairly.

I especially want to thank my great friends Goran Petersson from Sweden, Mary Pera from UK, Bill Bentsen from USA and Liv Sherwood from Canada. Some of these friends are eminent in the legal profession and kindly ignore my jibes about lawyers. I am jealous of their skills.

I am indebted to the many competitors, the vast majority of whom are much better sailors that I ever was who, with all the pressures from sponsors, parents with high aspirations, and the attraction of high monetary rewards have striven to play the game of yacht racing fairly, and when there is a dispute, to see the other man's point of view. They have provided my inspiration and rewards.

I am indebted to Tammi and Jae and Pip and Kim who have had to suffer the consequences of my spending so much time away from my family at championships and countless hours at home working on the word processor.

To my family and all my many friends, thank you.

*Bryan Willis*

# FOREWORD

## by Goran Petersson
## Vice President,
## International Yacht Racing Union

During the last ten years the sport of yachting has developed rapidly to become more exciting and more attractive to sponsors as well as sailors. More is now at stake. To win an important championship or a famous regatta may be the base for fame and sometimes also for fortune.

Sailing and tactical skill on the racecourse combined with physical fitness is no longer enough to win. An intimate knowledge of the racing rules and the ability to handle a protest hearing is also essential. The demands on the officials have followed suit.

The sport of yachting has its own judicial system to solve conflicts and to ensure fairness in the competition.

Many different situations arise – often rapidly – on the water during a yacht race. The rules must cover all these situations. They are therefore in many people's opinion complicated. Players and officials alike must, however, master the rules of the game.

Bryan Willis has for almost two decades during which he has been actively involved in the sport, been a respected and outspoken advocate of clarity of the rules and fairness for all. He has an exceptional experience as a rule maker, member of protest committees and international juries in all types of events from Optimist dinghies to the finals of the America's Cup and the Olympic Games as well as a yachtsman. He has also taken a great interest in improving the racing rules as a member of the IYRU racing rules committee. The IYRU judges system and its development has been a great beneficiary of his time and efforts for a long time. Teaching young people how to sail and compete is also one of his favourite subjects.

Bryan Willis has brought all the weight of his experience of yacht racing and his ability to observe, analyse and draw conclusions into this book.

The author's passion for challenges, his exceptional practical experience and ability to explain the meaning of the rules mix nicely in a work which contributes to a better knowledge and clearer picture of the proceeding for the practical handling of protests and appeals.

Bryan Willis has again made a generous contribution to the sport of yachting.

# INTRODUCTION

Twenty years ago, an Olympic medal or a world championship could be won without the need for boat-to-boat tactical battles. Tuning and sailing your boat faster than anyone else could often get you far enough ahead not to have to get involved with your immediate rivals. The overall winner would typically win many of the races that made up the series, sometimes by large margins. Knowing the intricacies of the racing rules was not very important, and many top sailors placed little importance on learning the rules that applied to the more complex boat-to-boat situations.

Things have changed. There are now so many good sailors with fast boats at the top of every international fleet that a championship series is often won without the winner ever being first across the finishing line. At every mark and on every offwind leg the leaders are now forced to be closely involved with their rivals.

A very good knowledge of rights and obligations in all but the rarest boat-to-boat situations has become essential for any sailor with aspirations of winning a championship.

By choice or chance, close manoeuvring sometimes leads to a collision or an incident in which both skippers think they are right, or at least are not sure they are wrong, and a protest ensues. Knowledge of the procedures then becomes important and sometimes vital. Every successful sailor will tell you about a coveted championship lost in the jury room.

This book is primarily for sailors who race competitively and want to be sure not to lose a race as a result of failing to adopt the correct or best procedure after an incident with another yacht or with the race committee. I hope too that the book will be useful for those serving on protest committees, whether they be racing sailors wanting to do a good job when appointed to serve on the occasional protest committee or have taken up judging as a vocation.

Bear in mind throughout the book that although the racing rules apply in the same way at a local week-end club race as they do at a world championship, a wise competitor will appreciate that a different approach and attitude is often required. When at a club event you are scored as having finished third when you know you came second, you go and see Raymond who was the race officer for the weekend and have a word with him. At a world championship you'd be wise to complete a written request for redress and lodge it before the end of protest time or as soon as you learn of the error.

Some of the procedures in the book deal with conflicts between competitor and race committee. I have assumed the reader is a competitor. Competitors make lots of mistakes and their race results suffer. Good race officers know that they too sometimes make mistakes, and that their mistakes sometimes prejudice the results of one or more competitors. When this happens good race officers are eager to find a solution. Not all race officers are good race officers, and much acrimony can develop when a competitor's chance of success is spoiled by a race official not willing to address himself to the effects of his error.

Most race officers know their responsibilities: to organise fair and enjoyable yacht racing. Competitors too have responsibilities: to play the game of yacht racing fairly; not to infringe a rule intentionally; having inadvertently infringed a rule to retire or take a penalty when challenged; and to co-operate with those who are involved with the organisation (race committee, protest committee, organising authority, etc.).

It is wrong to think that the race organisers are working solely for the competitors, though the best race officers are doubtless those who have the competitors' interests uppermost in their minds. All parties, whether they be competitors, race officers, judges, rescue and support personnel, and the yachting press, are all part of the sport of yacht racing; they all have their roles to play and they all have their responsibilities towards each other and to the sport.

# 1
# THE PARTIES

# 1  THE PARTIES

### The competitor, the yacht, and the yacht's representative

'Yacht racing' is an unfortunate term. 'Sailboat racing' would be better. 'Yacht racing' conjures up ideas of rich men racing in very expensive boats.[1] The vast majority of racing is done in sailing dinghies but as the racing rules were originally created for large sailing vessels, for the time being at any rate, we are stuck with the official term 'yacht racing' to describe all forms of sailboat racing, including radio-controlled models, children's single handed dinghies, sailboards, and the vast range of centreboard dinghies and keelboats.

However, it is worth noting how remarkable it is that all of these different kind of sailing vessels play more or less the same game: 'yacht racing'.

More important is the term 'yacht', which is used extensively throughout the rule book. It is usually what the boat itself does that matters, rather than what the skipper or crew do, or intend to do, or try to do. Yachts win races, yachts win trophies[2], yachts infringe rules, yachts lodge protests, yachts get penalised.

Even the rules governing the conduct of hearings speak of a yacht. 'A protesting yacht shall ....' or 'A yacht may...'. Of course, the yacht does not attended the hearing; the yacht is represented by its owner or a person appointed (explicitly or implicitly) by the owner. This person is called the yacht's 'representative', and is usually the skipper, but it can be anyone nominated by the owner, except that if the hearing is a protest alleging an infringement of a rule of parts IV or V (the sailing rules), then the representative must be someone who was on board at the time of the incident.[3]

The rules use the pronoun 'she', which of course relates to the yacht. In this book I'll use 'she' and 'her' to relate to the yacht, and merely to differentiate, 'him' and 'his' to relate to the skipper or owner, male or female.

So if the helmsman of a give-way yacht intends to bear away behind a right-of-way yacht, and tries hard to put the helm up to bear away but fails and there is contact, then it matters not that he tried, nor how hard he tried, nor that it was blowing hard and his mainsheet

[1] Things are changing. The United States Yacht Racing Union recently changed its name to US Sailing Association, and there's talk of the International Yacht Racing Union changing its name too.

[2] Sometimes, especially in events for dinghies, sailing instructions prescribe that points are accrued to the helmsman, in which case the helmsman wins the trophy

[3] Rule 73.

jammed; the yacht failed to keep clear. The only time a person or people's actions come under scrutiny is if they do something dishonourable, like lying in a hearing, or cheating in some other way. Only a yacht can infringe a sailing rule; only a person can cheat or behave badly.

Unless there is a sailing instruction which says that points will be awarded to the helmsman then it doesn't matter who helms the boat, and in a series of races any number of different people can take turns in helming or crewing; the points for race results being accrued by the yacht.[1]

## Protestor, protestee

The protestor is the yacht that lodges a protest. The person who attends the hearing and speaks on behalf of the protesting yacht is often referred to as the protestor, but strictly speaking is in fact the representative of the protestor. The protestee (not a word you'll find in the dictionary) is the yacht against which a protest has been lodged, and of course the person representing the yacht being protested is often referred to as the protestee.

## Parties to a protest

The protestor and the protestee are parties to the protest in which they are involved. If a third yacht becomes implicated and involved to the degree that she is, or might be, penalised at a hearing, then she becomes a party to the protest. In a redress hearing the requester is a party to the hearing. In a redress hearing where the race committee is involved, then provided that the body conducting the hearing is neither the race committee itself nor a committee appointed by the race committee, then the race committee is a party to the hearing. The significance of whether a yacht or a race committee is or is not a party to a protest is that only a party to a protest can appeal (provided the right to appeal has not been properly denied); a yacht which is not a party to a protest cannot appeal even though she may be affected by a protest committee's decision.[2]

## Witness

A witness is anyone who gives evidence at a hearing, about what he has seen or heard or knows in relation to an incident. The parties to the protest (the people representing the protestor and the protestee) are themselves witnesses. A member of the protest committee who gives evidence about what he or she saw of an incident is a witness. Someone called to give an opinion, perhaps on some technical matter, is also referred to as a witness even though he didn't actually see anything. The protestor, the protestee, the race committee if it is involved as a party, and the protest committee itself, all have the right to call any number of witnesses.

## Third yacht

A 'third yacht protest' is a colloquial term applied to a third yacht not involved in an incident but who protests one, or more usually both, of

[1] Sailing instructions often do prescribe that points are accrued by a person rather than the yacht, or that the yacht must be helmed by a particular person, especially in dinghy events. Class rules sometimes restrict who may helm (for example 'only paid-up members of the class association') or that permission from the jury is required for skipper/crew substitutions at major events.

[2] The yacht could request redress and, if not satisfied with the decision of that hearing, appeal.

the two yachts who are involved. The term is usually used in the context of a protest by a yacht who sees contact between two other yachts neither of which protests or retires or takes a penalty. The third yacht protests them both under rule 33 (which requires that when there is contact which is not both minor and unavoidable, one or both of the yachts shall protest or retire or take a penalty).

Whether or not you should protest when you see two other yachts make contact and neither protest or retire or take a penalty, is for you to decide. I never have; some always do; and it is certainly true to say that at championships, the majority do. You certainly have the right to do so provided you witness the infringement. (If you simply hear about it from someone on another yacht, you do not have the right to protest.)

The term 'third yacht' is also used to describe a yacht which is neither the protestor nor the protestee but is implicated in an incident. There may be a protest by A against B and at the hearing it becomes apparent to the committee that yacht C may be to blame. Yacht C (the 'third yacht') then become a party to the protests, and acquires the rights of a protestee, and may end up being disqualified, while A and B are 'acquitted'. How different to the procedures in a court of law!

## Interested party

An 'interested party' is defined in the racing rules as 'anyone who stands to gain or lose as a result of a decision of a protest committee or who has a close personal interest in the result'. The relevance of the term is that 'no member of a protest committee shall take part in the discussion or decision upon any disputed question in which he is an interested party, but this does not preclude him from giving evidence in such a case'. The rule (71.2) goes on to say 'A party to a protest who wishes to object to a member of the protest committee on the grounds that he is an interested party shall do so before evidence is taken at the hearing or as soon thereafter as he becomes aware of the conflict of interest'.

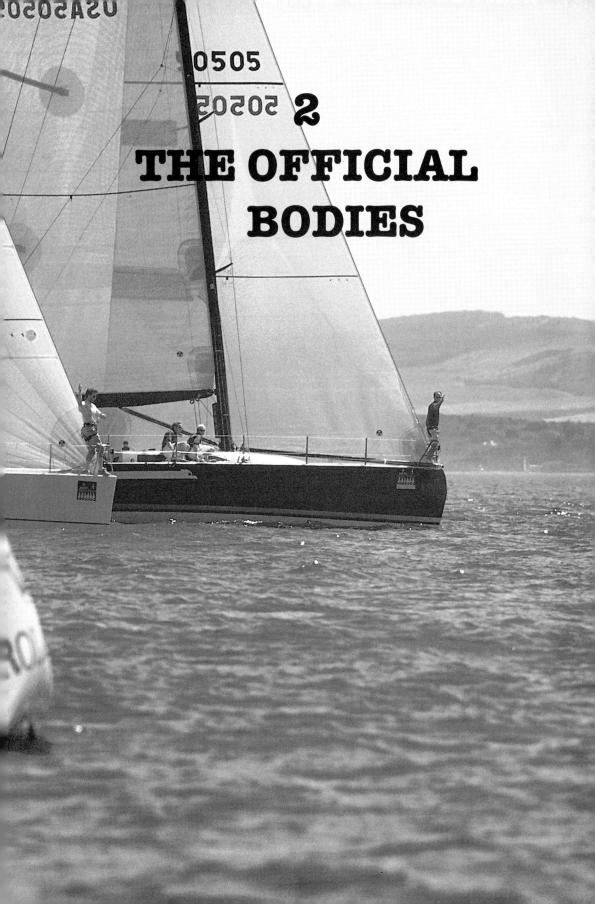

# 2
# THE OFFICIAL
# BODIES

# 2 THE OFFICIAL BODIES

## International Yacht Racing Union

The International Yacht Racing Union is the international authority overseeing yacht racing, and the racing rules. The IYRU comprises representatives of its member national authorities. International class associations and the Offshore Racing Council are affiliated to the IYRU, and there are several hundred personal members. The IYRU has a professional staff of about 12 headed by an Executive Director who reports to an executive committee consisting of the president and five vice presidents. The executive committee reports to the Council which comprises appointees from regions round the world.

There are many working committees which report to the Council, one of which is the racing rules committee. The RRC comprises 14 members appointed for their expertise and interest in the racing rules. There are never more than two members from any one nation. A core of about eight, mostly with English as their native tongue, form a permanent working party to work on the detail of proposals submitted by national authorities. The racing rules committee is responsible for processing rule change proposals submitted by national authorities and publishing a revised edition of the racing rules every four years (early in the year following the Olympic Games). It also considers for publication appeal cases decided and submitted by national authorities, but it never decides cases itself. If it disagrees with a national authority's decision submitted for consideration, it simply decides not to publish it.

So the role of the IYRU as far as hearings are concerned is simply as author of the procedures laid down in the rule book.

## National authority

Every nation where there is yacht racing has a national authority responsible for the administration of yacht racing within its jurisdiction. A few national authorities have a large staff of professionals responsible to an elected body of amateurs, but most are run by part-time or volunteer staff.

Approved clubs and other organising authorities within a national authority's jurisdiction become 'affiliated' to their national authority.

National authorities may add their own 'national prescriptions' to the racing rules. The major yacht racing nations publish their own racing rules booklets which contain the international yacht racing rules plus their national prescriptions printed in the relevant places.

National authorities are responsible for providing a system by which appeals can be processed (see Appeal authority).

## Organising authority

The organising authority is the body that decides to hold a race or series of races, and provides the venue. If it is not a national authority or the IYRU itself, the organising authority must be affiliated to a national authority or organise the event in conjunction with an affiliated body. The organising authority must appoint a race committee and publish a notice of race. If it is organising an international regatta, it might also appoint a jury or an international jury. The vast majority of organising authorities are sailing clubs and yacht clubs which organise one or more series of races each season When a club appoints a sailing committee and publishes its annual programme, it is in fact appointing a race committee and publishing a notice of race.

## Race committee

The organising authority must appoint a race committee to run the races and publish the results. Part II of the International Yacht Racing Rules describes the obligations of the race committee. The race committee must publish 'sailing instructions' describing its intentions with respect to classes, race times, courses, starting and finishing lines, and the scoring system to be used, together with any additional obligations of yachts and their crews.

When the race committee fails to comply with the obligations placed on it by the racing rules, or fails to carry out its intentions prescribed by its own sailing instructions, it opens the possibility, and in major events I would say probability, of yachts requesting redress.

## Protest committee

'Protest committee' is a general term. A protest committee might be the race committee sitting to hear a protest, or a sub-committee appointed by the race committee to conduct a hearing, or a jury or an international jury which not only conducts hearings, but goes out on the water to monitor rule observance, and might be given other responsibilities. Any legitimate committee conducting a protest hearing, or a redress hearing, is a 'protest committee'.

The racing rules do not require a minimum number of members for a protest committee unless it's an international jury. Interestingly, one of the two definitions of 'committee' in the Oxford Dictionary is 'a person to whom a function is committed'[1]. However, it is unusual for a protest committee to comprise less than three people.

[1] The pronunciation is different: the emphasis is on the 'tee'

When the two yachts involved in a protest were racing in separate races each with its own organising authority, the protest committee

[1] Rule 71.3

membership must include someone appointed by each of the organising authorities.[1]

## Jury

A jury is a protest committee independent of the race committee. It is appointed by the organising authority. Typically a jury is appointed for an open regatta, or an area, regional or national championship. There is no minimum number of members of a jury; usually there are three members.

## International jury

[2] Some classes require an organising authority running their world championship to appoint an international jury.

An organising authority is not *required* to appoint an international jury[2] but may choose to do so at a major international event in the hope of giving a better service to competitors, making those from abroad feel more comfortable, and to avoid the problems at the prize-giving that can occur if an appeal is pending. There must be a minimum of five members (unless reduced by illness or an emergency), the majority of whom must be international Judges (appointed by the IYRU), and not more than two may be from any one nation. Provided that it acts within its terms of reference (described in Racing Rules Appendix A5), decisions made by an international jury are not open to appeal.

## Appeal authority

It is up to each national authority to decide how it is to discharge its obligation to provide an appeals service. Some have permanent appeals committees; some smaller nations appoint an appeals committee on the rare occasion when they receive an appeal; some use another nation's appeal committee. The International Yacht Racing Union does not hear appeals; the ultimate appeal authority is the national authority of the organising authority in whose jurisdiction the event took place.

In countries other than the United States of America and Canada, there is only one appeal level; that is, having exhausted any possibilities with the protest committee at the event itself, there is only the national authority to appeal to (and even this is denied when there is a properly constituted international jury acting within its jurisdiction, or sometimes when the event is of a type where yachts doing well in early races qualify to sail in later races).

# 3
# TYPES OF
# HEARING

# 3 TYPES OF HEARING

The system of processing protests and other grievances resulting from incidents in a yacht race is a service to competitors. No one likes protests; they often cause people to get upset, they delay the results, they consume time which could be better spent in merriment. But when you've been involved in an incident and you feel aggrieved about it, you need this service.

A hearing is a formal procedure in which a committee listens to evidence, assesses and decides on validity, finds facts, and makes a decision. There are several types of hearing, the protest hearing being the most common. The requirements needing to be satisfied for each type of hearing to be valid differ considerably. An invalid protest or request cannot proceed and must be 'refused', a valid protest or request must proceed and will, after a hearing, be 'upheld' or 'dismissed'.

The procedure is the same, whether the incident happened at a small club in the Tuesday evening race resulting in the once-in-a-year protest, or in a championship to decide the world champion.

Sometimes a yacht lodges a protest when she should be requesting redress. The skipper might have ticked the wrong box on the form. A good protest committee will recognise this and simply accept the protest form as though it were a request for redress and proceed accordingly, applying the relevant tests for validity.

## Protest hearing, yacht v yacht

The most usual type of hearing is the yacht versus yacht protest hearing, in which one yacht protests another yacht. However, a yacht may protest several other yachts, or several yachts may protest one yacht. In either case, if the protest relates to a single incident, then a single hearing would normally be appropriate. The requirements to be satisfied for a protest to be valid include a hail, the prompt and conspicuous display of a protest flag, and timely lodging of a written document[1].

[1] The sailing instructions may increase or reduce these requirements.

## Protest hearing - committee v yacht

The race committee (or the protest committee if there is one) may protest a yacht or any number of yachts, but just as a yacht has to satisfy certain requirements for her protest to be valid, so must the committee, though the validity requirements are not so onerous. The committee does not have to inform the yacht immediately after the incident (which means the yacht might be deprived of the opportunity to exonerate herself by taking a penalty). The committee does have to inform the yacht in writing, by 1800 the following day.

Neither the race committee nor the protest committee is ever obliged to protest or initiate a hearing [1]. It is usually appropriate for it to do so when the alleged infringement involves serious damage, or the perpetrator has gained a significant advantage, or when the sport might be brought into disrepute by action not being taken.

There is nothing in the rules to compel a race committee to appoint a separate protest committee (when there isn't already one appointed) to hear the case, but if its own conduct is the subject of the case, justice will not be seen to be done if it doesn't.

So the party (or parties) initiating a case may be a yacht, or several yachts, or the race committee, or the protest committee, or a jury. The 'protestee' (the defendant) is always a yacht (or yachts) (except in a Rule 75 hearing when the protestee is always a person).

## Measurement protest hearing

At major events, an official measurer is sometimes appointed. A measurer may check the yachts comply with their class or measurement rules. Unlike the discretion given to a protest committee as to whether or not to initiate a hearing when it sees an infringement, the official measurer has some very definite powers and responsibilities. Where something is wrong and can be put right before a race, he *must* request the owner to correct the defect, failing which he *must* report the matter to the race committee which *must* reject or rescind the entry [2]. When he concludes after a race that the yacht does not comply with her class rules, the measurer *must* inform the protest committee, and the protest committee must call a hearing.[3]

A yacht may protest another yacht when there is evidence of a measurement infringement, and of course when the protest committee receives a valid protest from a yacht, the protest committee must proceed with a hearing.

Having heard the evidence, if the protest committee is in 'no reasonable doubt' as to the 'interpretation or application' of the measurement rule, it may decide the case, either dismissing it or penalising the yacht. When the committee is in doubt, it *must* refer the question to 'an authority qualified to resolve such question'. This would normally be the measurement committee of the class. Having received the authority's ruling, the protest committee must be governed by it.[4]

## Redress hearing

When a yacht claims her finishing position (in a race or a series) has been materially prejudiced by an 'improper action' of the race committee (or the protest committee), she may 'seek redress'. The

[1] There is an exception. When an official measurer concludes that a yacht does not comply with her class rules or measurement or rating certificate (Rule 70.4)

[2] The yacht can ask for a hearing

[3] Rule 70.4

[4] Rule 74.3

process is sometimes (wrongly) called 'protesting the race committee'. Some examples: the race committee sets a course that is misunderstood by some yachts that sail a course different to the rest of the fleet; a buoy is moved as yachts are sailing towards it; an error is made in calculating the final scores in a series.

A yacht may also seek redress when her finishing position has been materially prejudiced after giving assistance to a person or yacht in distress (which Fundamental Rule A compels her to do), or when she is physically damaged by another vessel (which is usually, but not always, a sailing yacht) which was required to keep clear (by either the racing rules or the collision regulations), or for one or two other more unusual reasons[1].

[1] See rule 69(b) and (d)

When the claim for redress meets the requirements, the protest committee is required to 'make as equitable an arrangement as possible for all yachts concerned'. This usually means giving the claimant points equal to an artificial finishing position. Rarely would the committee's obligation be satisfied by declaring a race void.

## Hearing to investigate a starting or finishing infringement

Because the race committee may score as 'did not start' or 'did not finish' a yacht without a hearing for failing to start or finish, the rules give the right to a yacht thus penalised to request a hearing to investigate a claim that she was wrongly penalised. On receipt of such a request, the race committee must arrange a hearing (or having realised it has made an error, put the matter right). The rules are not clear as to whether the race committee may conduct its own hearing when a jury has been appointed, but it is usual for the protest committee to conduct all hearings.

A request for a hearing can be made orally, but if there is doubt as to whether the request will be acted upon, then it is best to submit it in writing.

## Hearing to investigate a rule 54 disqualification

At dinghy championships, sailing instructions often prescribe that the protest committee may disqualify without a hearing a yacht it considers has infringed rule 54 (Propulsion). Typically this is when there is a protest committee that takes on the job of sending pairs of observers afloat in motor boats to record rule 54 infringements using tape recorders. A member of the protest committee or one of its appointed observers must have actually seen the infringement; the committee cannot disqualify a yacht on hearsay evidence. The disqualification is usually indicated in the race results, so when there is a sailing instruction prescribing this procedure, it is important for competitors to inspect the results.

A yacht thus disqualified is entitled to a hearing on request. This is best done in writing and submitted to the race office. For example 'Yacht 12345 requests a hearing in respect of the disqualification for an alleged infringement of rule 54 in race number 3, signed Ivor Grievance, time and date'.

When the protest committee was the body that disqualified the yacht in the first place, it may seem unjust that it will now be hearing the case, especially since at the commencement of the hearing the yacht is 'guilty' and will remain so unless she can establish her 'innocence'. Those members of the committee who saw the infringement must give the evidence which led to the disqualification, and the yacht's representative, using any witnesses and his own evidence, must establish either that the yacht wasn't doing what the committee witnesses say she was doing, or that what she was doing didn't infringe rule 54.

If the yacht succeeds (which happens occasionally), the decision to disqualify is reversed; otherwise the decision to disqualify is simply confirmed.

## Re-opened hearing

A yacht may request that a hearing be re-opened, but for the request to be upheld (and a hearing reopened) the yacht must have been a 'party to the protest' (a protestor or a protestee or subjected to a penalty). Furthermore, the yacht must satisfy the protest committee either that 'it may have made a significant error' (from the requester's point of view of course that means the protest committee has penalised him and it should have penalised the other yacht or dismissed the protest), or that material new evidence has become available within a reasonable time.[1] The request must be received by 1800 on the day following the original decision (although the committee can extend this time limit).

When these requirements have not been satisfied the protest committee cannot re-open the hearing. Conversely, although the rules don't say as much, natural justice requires that when the requirements *have* been satisfied, the protest committee *must* re-open the hearing.

Without a request from a party, the committee can decide to re-open a hearing when the requirements have been met.

Often, a decision by a protest committee indirectly affects other yachts. For example, redress might be given to a yacht by giving her an artificial finishing position, and this adversely affects the overall standing of other yachts. One of these yachts might request a re-opening with the objective of convincing the committee that the redress it gave was too generous or ill-conceived. However, as these yachts were not party to the original protest they have no right to request a re-opening. However, they could request redress, and a sensible committee would accept a re-opening request as a request for redress.

[1] Material new evidence is evidence that it is likely to have an effect on the outcome of a protest (material) and that wasn't available at the time of the original hearing (new).

## 'Rule 75' hearing

When a protest committee has reasonable grounds for believing that a competitor has committed 'a gross infringement of the rules' or 'a gross breach of good manners or sportsmanship', it may call a hearing to investigate the matter. The decision to proceed is often made after receiving a report from another competitor or an official.

A yacht or competitor cannot protest another competitor for 'infringing rule 75'. In fact rule 75 cannot actually be infringed because it doesn't actually place an obligation on a competitor or a yacht. However, a competitor (or a spectator or anyone else) can inform the protest committee (or race committee if there is no protest committee) when there is evidence of cheating or offensive behaviour, and the committee can initiate a hearing. Since heavy penalties can be imposed, it would be foolish not to comply with the implied obligations in rule 75: to act at all times in a sportsmanlike way, not infringe rules intentionally in an attempt to gain an unfair advantage, and behave reasonably.

Although the protest committee has considerable discretion when it comes to imposing a penalty, and all or part of the penalty might be imposed on a yacht rather than the person concerned, the 'protestee' is always a person or people.

Some examples of the type of behaviour that have been the subject of rule 75 hearings are: cheating (such as shifting ballast in a keelboat), knowingly omitting to round a mark, lying at a hearing, fighting on and off the water, and using language that causes offence.

Sometimes there is no penalty, though the committee might give a warning. If a penalty is given it can be as much as disqualification from the entire regatta or series. When a penalty is imposed, it has to be reported to the national authorities of the event, the competitor, and the yacht, and those national authorities may extend the penalty, for example by suspending a competitor's eligibility within the area under the jurisdiction of the national authority. The International Yacht Racing Union may then extend the suspension worldwide.

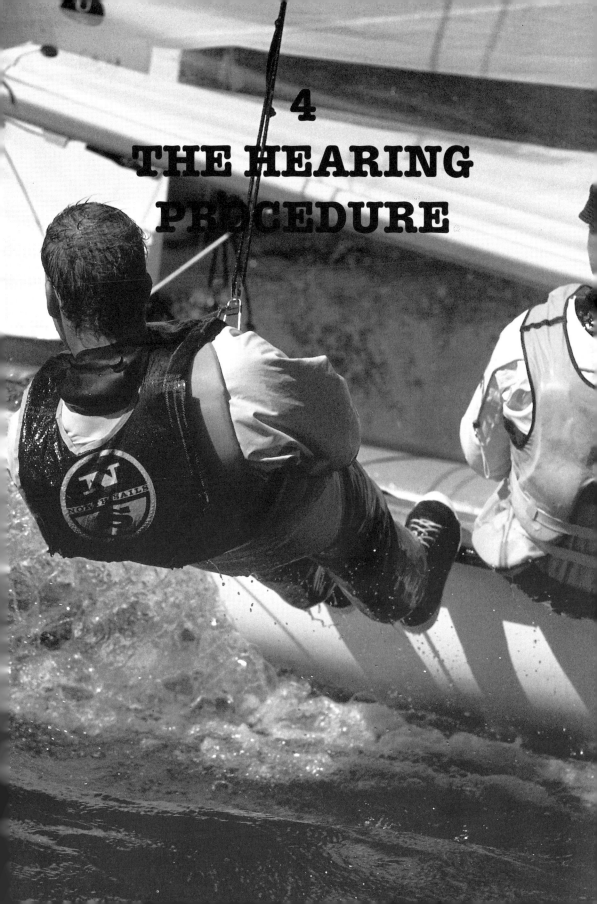

# 4
# THE HEARING PROCEDURE

# 4 THE HEARING PROCEDURE

The general procedure for any type of hearing is fairly standard. The committee members meet and read the documents. The parties are called in. Evidence about validity is heard and a decision made as to whether the protest or request is valid. If valid, evidence about the case itself is heard from the parties and witnesses who are questioned by the parties and committee members. The committee makes its decision in private. The parties are recalled and the decision is announced.

## The protest room

Most yacht clubs and sailing clubs have a 'committee room' which is used (amongst many other things) for the conduct of hearings. At championships, several rooms are sometimes needed including a room where parties and witnesses can wait.

The members of the committee sit in a row behind a table with the chairman in the middle. The parties, and each witness when called to give evidence, will sit opposite them. There are often models or a blackboard or flip-chart to help the parties and other witnesses to give their evidence.

Ideally, the committee room (or jury room, as it is called when a jury has been appointed) is quiet, with soundproof walls, big enough to seat everyone comfortably, ventilated, and not too hot or cold!

## Members of the protest committee

The committee is likely to comprise three members (a chairman plus two). If it is sitting to hear a request for redress, its membership should be independent of the race committee. If it is hearing a protest its members might be the same as those of the race committee.

At a championship the protest committee is likely to be a jury appointed by the organising authority, and have a membership of three or five.

At an international championship, it is likely to be an international jury with five members.

## 'Interested party' as a member of the committee

No one is allowed to sit on the protest committee if he is an 'interested party'. The rules define an 'interested party' as 'anyone who stands to

gain or lose as a result of a decision of a protest committee or who
has a close personal interest in the result'.[1]

[1] Rule 71.2 (a)

At the level of regattas where international juries are appointed, an
'interested party' is a rarity. However, organising authorities
sometimes unwisely appoint a competitor's parent or relative as a
member of a jury; as the results of almost every hearing would
directly effect that competitor's score, the appointee would have to
stand down for all those hearings.

As a competitor it is important that you question 'interest' as soon as
you are aware of it.[2] A good protest committee chairman will address
any possibility of interest before the hearing begins, but if he doesn't,
and you know about a committee member who you think fulfils the
definition of 'interested party', you must consider whether you are
prepared to accept the situation, and if not, you must raise the
question immediately. To make this the point, or even a point, of an
appeal is unlikely to lead to the appeal being upheld if you didn't
make a timely complaint. So when you have lodged a protest against
John and the chairman says to you 'We are having difficulty finding
sufficient experienced people to serve on the protest committee;
Mary here is John's Aunt; are you prepared to accept Mary as a
member of the committee?', and you answer 'yes', then that is an end
of the matter. By the way, you shouldn't jump to the conclusion that
Mary will favour John in the committee's deliberations; she might be
so keen to be unbiased, she actually leans the other way!

[2] Rule 71.2 (b)

## Observers

At any level of event, observers are sometimes allowed to attend a
hearing. Whether or not observers are permitted to sit in on hearings,
and the extent to which they are positively encouraged to do so, is for
the committee itself to decide. Observers usually sit to one side, and
a little away from the table. They are not permitted to speak or
disturb the proceedings in any way. The committee chairman should
ensure that none of the observers is involved in or witnessed the
incident.

If you are a party to the protest and you are going to call witnesses,
make sure none of them is in the group of observers.

If you are uncomfortable with the presence of observers, you can
ask for the hearing to be conducted without them, but you may have
to provide a reason, and your request might be refused by the
committee. The presence of observers (provided they are well
behaved!) usually enhances the respect for the work of the protest
committee, and personally I think allowing observers is usually
beneficial, provided there is space for them.

At junior events, I strongly recommend that an adult supporter for
each of the parties be encouraged to attend as an observer. At
Optimist World Championships (where the skippers are all-under

16), a coach or team leader sits behind and to the side of each of the two parties. They remain silent throughout (unless they are needed as translators). The huge benefit is that they see that their skipper has had a fair hearing; in their absence they could never be sure this was the case.

At an America's Cup there might be unacceptable pressures put on the participants were the press be allowed to watch hearings and, as far as I know, observers have never been allowed.

## Date and time of hearing

The protest committee must inform the parties of the time and place of the hearing.[1] At a club event this can be done orally. At a championship parties can be informed orally, but championship sailing instructions often prescribe a system of notification using the official notice board which means you must check at the close of protest time whether you are involved, since you cannot rely on being informed in any other way. However, without a special sailing instruction, the committee must inform you personally, although if you are the protestor you must make a reasonable effort to find out when and where your protest will be heard.

If the race committee or protest committee is initiating a hearing against you, you must be given a written copy of the protest.[2]

If another yacht is protesting you, you are entitled to see the written protest or to be given a copy of it.[3]

At championships where hearings are to be expected, you can expect them to be scheduled promptly after the day's racing. At a sailing club, arranging a hearing arising from a club race is sometimes not so easy. There is often the need for a compromise between holding the hearing soon after the race when everyone's memory is fresh but with the protest committee comprising people who were competing in the race, or with those who didn't race but have little racing experience on the protest committee, and waiting several days or a week for more experienced or independent committee members, when memories are fading. In my opinion, it is best to have a hearing soon after the race, at least to establish the facts.

## Validity

Each type of hearing has its own validity requirements. Before a hearing can progress to the point when evidence about the incident is heard, the committee must decide whether or not it is valid. Although on some questions of validity the protest committee has some discretion, when the requirements are met the protest committee must decide that the protest or request is 'valid' and proceed with the hearing. When the requirements are not met the protest committee must decide the protest or request is 'invalid' and state the reason why it is invalid, and must 'refuse' it.

[1] Rule 72

[2] Rule 70.2

[3] Rule 72

The process of addressing and deciding on whether or not a protest or request is valid usually takes a few seconds, but sometimes it can be a long and complicated procedure, especially if one of the parties (the protestee in the case of a protest) disputes the validity. But even when the protestee readily accepts that a protest is valid, the committee still has the duty to satisfy itself that it is valid. The validity requirements cannot be set aside just because the protestee is prepared to proceed.

Witnesses might have to be heard and cross-examined just on the question of validity, before the actual hearing ever gets started, if indeed it does. Many protests are ruled as invalid and refused.

## Withdrawing a protest

When a yacht hails 'protest' and displays a protest flag, she reserves the right to lodge a protest, but hailing and displaying does not commit her to actually lodging it.

Lodging means handing the written protest to an official. Generally, once a protest is lodged it cannot be withdrawn. There are two exceptions, which I will explain now, but the second of these two exceptions is hardly worth knowing about.

### Acknowledging the infringement

When one of the parties 'acknowledges the infringement' before the hearing starts, the protest isn't exactly withdrawn, but it has to be set aside.[1] When a protestee is unsure whether he infringed the rule he is accused of infringing in the protest form, apart from saving time, there is not much incentive to 'acknowledge the infringement', as the difference between the points awarded for a late retirement and points awarded for a disqualification after a hearing is usually insignificant. 'Acknowledging the infringement' means acknowledging having infringed the rule that has been alleged to have been infringed in the protest form, not merely retiring for an unspecified reason.[2]

[1] Rule 68.8

[2] See section on insurance claims and damage

### Protestor wanting to withdraw her protest

When two yachts collide but the contact is both minor and unavoidable, there is no joint obligation on the two yachts for one of them to protest or take a penalty (or retire).[3] From the point of view of that obligation it is just as if there had been no contact.[4]

So in the rare case of contact which is both minor and unavoidable and when neither yacht wants to protest, neither need take any action, but if a third yacht sees the contact and being of the opinion that the contact was not 'minor and unavoidable' lodges a protest against both yachts for infringing rule 33 (the rule that obliges at least one of two yachts to protest or retire), there is a possibility that the committee will find that the contact was not minor and unavoidable, uphold the third yacht's protest, and disqualify both protestees.

[3] Rule 33

[4] There is, of course, an obligation on a yacht that knows she has infringed, to retire or take a penalty. When there is a collision, albeit a minor and unavoidable one, there is an infringement and it is usually obvious to both yachts which yacht has infringed. In practice, without a complaint by the right-of-way yacht, the give-way yacht does not even consider taking a penalty.

The committee will not go into which yacht was right-of-way and which was give-way; it will simply address whether there was contact and if there was, whether it was minor and unavoidable. If it finds as a fact that there was contact and that it was not minor and unavoidable, it will decide that both yachts infringed rule 33 and disqualify both. On the other hand if it finds there was no contact or that there was contact but that it was 'minor and unavoidable' then it will dismiss the third yacht's protest.

Fearful of a 'third yacht protest' and the committee finding as a fact that the contact was not minor and unavoidable, one of the two yachts involved in the contact (typically the one that thinks she was the right-of-way yacht) may lodge a protest but argue that the contact was minor and unavoidable. Should the committee agree, then she is permitted to withdraw the protest. Should the committee find that there was contact and that it was not minor and unavoidable, then the protestor's protest can proceed (under some other rule of part IV) and the committee must consider which right-of-way rule was infringed and disqualify the infringing yacht.

A few words about the term 'minor and unavoidable'. Minor and unavoidable collisions are rare. Minor means a light touch. Unavoidable means that try as she might, through no fault of her own, a yacht has so little steerage way that even though she is at a distance where she is 'keeping clear', she is drawn to the other yacht, perhaps by waves, or some mystical attraction between floating vessels.

'Minor and unavoidable' can never be used as a defence in a protest, except when the protest is brought by a third yacht claiming an infringement (by two yachts) of rule 33, or brought by one of the two yachts not actually wanting to protest but fearful of a third yacht protesting.

It is important to appreciate that whenever there is contact, albeit minor and unavoidable, there is always an infringement of some rule of part IV.[1]

[1] There are some exceptions when a yacht helps another in distress, or unavoidably collides with a capsized yacht

In twenty years judging I've never come across a case where a protestor wanted to withdraw her protest because she claimed the contact was minor and unavoidable.

## Evidence, facts, and the decision

In the language of the racing rules, evidence is everything a witness (and that includes the parties) says or shows in a hearing to the committee. John says 'My yacht Ostrobogulous was on starboard tack'; that is evidence. Had John said 'It is an indisputable fact agreed by both parties that my yacht Ostrobogulous was on starboard tack', that too would be evidence, not a fact. John places a model on the table with its boom on a particular side, in a particular position in relation to other models; that is evidence. If John were to bring in his damaged rudder for the committee to see, then the damaged rudder would be evidence. Descriptions and diagrams in a written protest form are evidence. When John says 'Bill told me after the race that he definitely saw that I was on starboard tack at the time of contact', that is evidence (but without Bill, is valueless). An opinion given at a hearing by a measurer or some other specialist is evidence. A video recording is evidence. Photographs are evidence (but usually of little value). A written report from someone not able to attend a hearing is hearsay evidence, and without its author available to answer questions about it, it too is of limited value.

Only the committee finds facts, based on the evidence, almost always in private, and only after a valid hearing. If it decides 'Obstrobogulous was on port tack' then that becomes a fact. Whether it was true or not is another matter. Facts found by the protest committee are not open to appeal. It is therefore far more important to provide the evidence which will lead the committee to find what you consider to be the facts which reflect what you think actually happened, than to guide them in applying the correct rules.

The decision (for example to disqualify Ostrobogulous) is also made by the committee and must be based on the facts found. Should the decision not be the correct one based on the facts, then an aggrieved party can successfully appeal (unless the right to appeal has been denied for a legitimate reason).

A party cannot appeal the facts themselves, as the appeal authority cannot change the facts found by the protest committee. If a fact was found which was totally unreasonable, an appeal authority might return the case to the committee for reconsideration or comment.

## Onus of proof

The term 'onus of proof' is often used (wrongly) in place of the term used in the rule book: 'onus of satisfying the protest committee'.

A protestor must satisfy the committee that an infringement occurred or at least might have occurred. So a protest claiming that a yacht is 'illegal' (that is, that it infringes a class rule) would have to include a reason why the protestor thinks there has been an infringement. Just because the accused yacht is the fastest on the racecourse would be insufficient. This prime obligation for the protestor is not described in the rule book (although in my opinion it should be) but there are several examples in appeal decisions. In the vast majority of cases it is not a point to be questioned, as there is sufficient evidence (usually in the protest form) to convince the protest committee that there 'may have been an infringement' (or, to put it another way, there is 'a case to answer'.)

Members of the protest committee should take an active role in questioning the witnesses so that the 'facts found' are as close to what actually happened as possible. Although the protest committee is not obliged to do so, not to take an active role in questioning the witnesses would give an experienced or legally trained party a big advantage over one who was not. Protest hearings are not courts of law; we don't have a prosecution and defence.

There are just four situations described in the rule book where there is an 'onus of satisfying the protest committee'. They are:

Tacking or gybing close to another yacht. The tacking (or gybing) yacht has the onus of satisfying the protest committee that she completed her tack (or gybe) far enough from the other yacht to enable her to keep clear without having to begin to alter course until after the tack or gybe was completed.[1]

[1] Rule 41.3

Room at a mark - breaking an overlap. The yacht claiming the overlap was broken has the onus of satisfying the protest committee that she became clear ahead when she was more than two of her overall lengths from the mark.[2]

[2] Rule 42.1 (c)

Room at a mark - establishing a late overlap. The yacht claiming an inside overlap has the onus of satisfying the protest committee that the overlap was established in proper time.[3]

[3] Rule 42.1 (d)

A yacht choosing not to tack in response to a hail at an obstruction. A yacht that replies 'you tack' the onus of satisfying the protest committee that she gave sufficient room.[4]

[4] Rule 43.2 (b)(iii)

When any of these four situations is an issue, rather than sit back and see whether the party can satisfy the committee, a good committee will take an active role in questioning the parties, and if in spite of their answers, the committee is unsure, then, and only then, will it 'go with the onus' and decide that 'the protest committee is not satisfied'.

## The decision-making process

When the parties have given the evidence they want to give, the decision-making process begins. The committee does this in private, so the parties are asked to leave. If there are observers, they too are asked to leave. Alternatively, the committee members retire to somewhere where they can discuss the case in private.

The committee must 'find facts' by considering the evidence presented at the hearing. It can put what weight it likes on the various pieces of testimony. The committee might believe one party who brought no witnesses and disbelieve the other who brought many. It might be inclined to rate as 'low quality' evidence from someone who the committee believes is a perpetual 'truth stretcher'. Since the committee discusses the case in private, and writes the 'facts found' without having to justify what it finds, the members can discuss anything they think is relevant, including the quality of evidence and credibility of witnesses.

## Coming to an agreement

When they go into their private decision-making mode, the committee members discuss the evidence they have heard. If one of them witnessed the incident, he is not permitted to say any more than he said in the hearing. There is rarely the necessity for a vote, as a member holding a minority view is usually happy to be persuaded by the others, but if there is disagreement about an important point they will discuss the evidence relating to that point. Unless a committee member feels so strongly that the others are wrong that he dissociates himself from the decision, you will never know whether the 'facts found' and decision were agreed on unanimously or by a majority.

## Giving the decision

When the committee has agreed on 'facts found' and made its decision based on those facts as to which yacht(s) (if any) infringed a rule, and what the penalty will be (there is usually no alternative open to the committee but disqualification from the race), the parties are recalled and the decision read out. If you don't understand some part of the decision, you can ask for clarification, but few chairmen will allow a discussion.

## When a party doesn't show up

When one of the parties fails to come to the hearing, the protest committee has to consider whether proper notice was given. If not, it might postpone the hearing to another time or date. If it believes proper notice was given, or that the party (usually the protestee) has no intention of coming, then it will proceed with the hearing. Provided that the evidence given by the protestor (and his witnesses) is believed by the committee and includes an infringement by the protestee, the protest will be upheld, and the protestee penalised. If it is the protestor that fails to attend, and the protestee's evidence is believed and includes an infringement by the protestor, then the protestor will be penalised, so it is most unwise for a protestor not to attend! If both parties fail to attend, then evidence from witnesses (including members of the protest committee if any of them saw the incident) can be heard and will determine the outcome. If neither party attends and there are no witnesses, then the case has to be dismissed as there is no evidence. The protest form itself is not evidence but simply an allegation which, without any supporting evidence, is of no value, even if it includes an allegation of contact.

# 5
# PROTESTING &
# DEFENDING
# A PROTEST

# 5 PROTESTING & DEFENDING A PROTEST

This section is very much for you, the sailor. It describes your rights, and gives some advice.

## The right to protest

A yacht has the right to lodge a protest against another yacht (or other yachts) only when she (the protesting yacht) is involved in the incident, or witnesses the incident. So if you hear someone at the bar talking about an incident, or you hear a collision between two boats (not including yours) at a crowded windward mark but see nothing, you cannot lodge a protest (or at least, if you do, it will be ruled as invalid).

If you see what you think is an infringement, you can protest the yacht or yachts you believe have infringed. The alleged infringement might be in relation to one or more racing rule, or a sailing instruction, or class rule, or national prescription. If your protest is valid it must be heard (the protest committee has no right to refuse it).

If you simply suspect that a yacht has infringed shall we say a measurement rule but you haven't 'witnessed an incident' you have no right to protest, but you could inform the measurer if there is one, and action might be taken, but your report has no significance under the rules because you are an interested party.[1]

[1] Rule 70.4 permits a measurer to report to the protest committee which must call a hearing.

You cannot protest people, only yachts. If you believe a competitor has cheated, or committed a gross breach of good sportsmanship, or a gross breach of the rules, or a gross breach of good manners, your only way of bringing the culprit to account is to report the matter to the protest committee (or the race committee if no protest committee has been appointed). The protest committee is not obliged to initiate a hearing, but if you persuade the committee that there are reasonable grounds for believing such an offence has occurred, it is certainly in the best interests of the sport if the committee does initiate a hearing (under rule 75). You might be asked to attend, especially if you are involved, but you are not a protestor, simply a witness; the case is brought by the committee.

If you retire (you may be forced to retire by being damaged), you may never-the-less protest. If you retire because you think you have infringed a rule (and there are no alternative penalties available in the sailing instructions), or if you think you have infringed a rule and take an alternative penalty, or even if you don't think you've infringed a rule and you take a penalty, you are still permitted to protest. So retiring in acknowledgement of an infringement does not prevent you from protesting (provided you meet the requirements for a protest to be valid).

A 'third yacht' protest by a yacht who sees contact between two other yachts is common in championships. The third yacht protests them both under rule 33 (which requires that when there is contact which is not both minor and unavoidable, one or both of the yachts shall protest or retire or take a penalty).

Although many competitors don't realise it, the 'third yacht protest' is not limited to rule 33. Even when rule 33 is the main reason for protesting, an astute third yacht will add a rule of part IV section B to his protest (for example rule 37.1 'windward to keep clear of leeward', or rule 36 'port tack to keep clear of starboard tack'). Then if the protest committee finds as a fact that there was no contact, or that contact was minor and unavoidable, it will dismiss the alleged infringement of rule 33, but must then address itself to the claim that rule 37.1 or 36 or whatever it is, has been infringed, and if it decides that such an infringement has occurred, it must disqualify the infringing yacht.

There is no obligation on you to lodge a protest if you are not involved in a collision. If you are on starboard tack and you choose to duck under the stern of a yacht on port tack, you are not required to protest. You may see a clear-cut infringement by another yacht, but you are not required to protest.

There are 'right to protest' rules also for the race committee and the protest committee (or jury if one has been appointed). For the race committee (or protest committee or jury) to initiate a hearing ('protest a yacht'), it must have seen an incident. When I say 'it must have seen' I mean any one of the committee's members, or its agents. So if the man on the committee boat in charge of flags sees an infringement, the race committee could protest the yacht, even if the flag man is not actually a member of the race committee, as he is obviously an agent of the committee. The same would be true of the mark-boat driver, or anyone else acting on behalf of the race committee. The individual cannot protest the yacht, he simply informs the committee what he has seen. Whether or not the race or protest committee proceeds with a protest when it receives a report from one or more of its members or agents, is a committee decision. It is the committee as a body that lodges the protest.

The spectator boat driver who is under the direction of the organising authority is probably not an agent of the race committee so when he sees an infringement, it is not as if the race committee has seen it. However, provided that he is not an interested party, he may submit a report to the race committee and they may initiate a hearing based on that report. The race committee may not act on a report from any party that has an interest in a particular yacht or group of yachts (from a particular nation, for example).

The same principles apply to a protest committee or a jury. If it has appointed observers, then the observers are its agents and if they see an apparent infringement, then it is as if the protest committee or jury has seen it.

[1] Rule 70.2

There are some other situations where the race committee or protest committee may 'protest' a yacht.[1]

The protest committee is never obliged to proceed with a protest after witnessing an incident, although if it is the type of incident which affects the fairness of the competition it should do so. The policy about when it should protest and when it should not, is a very important one. A race committee that does not protest a yacht when it sees a blatant infringement which gained the infringer places in the race, brings the sport into disrepute and abrogates respect for the race committee. On the other hand a wise race committee will not protest a port tack yacht in a 'port and starboard' incident when there was no contact and the starboard tack yacht chose not to protest.

## When you should protest

Some competitors protest at every opportunity, whether they are sailing in a world championship or a local club Wednesday evening race, and whether the yacht they are protesting is being sailed by an expert or a beginner. They are not popular, and I don't recommend such a policy.

There are two situations in which a yacht must lodge a protest in that by not lodging one she herself infringes a rule and becomes liable to disqualification or other penalty.

One is when two yachts make contact (when it is other than 'minor and unavoidable' which is very unusual); one or other (or both) yachts must either lodge a valid protest or retire or, if the facility for taking an alternative penalty has been prescribed in the sailing instructions, take an alternative penalty. So if your yacht has a collision with another yacht, and the other yacht does not retire or take a penalty or protest, then you are required to protest (or retire or take a penalty); failure to do so may prompt a third yacht or the race or protest committee to protest both of you, resulting in both of you being disqualified at the hearing.

If there is a collision and you think you were in the right, and the other yacht does not take a penalty or retire and shouts 'protest' and displays a protest flag, you could decide simply to defend the protest against you, and if you are successful in that respect, then the other yacht will be disqualified (even though there was no protest against her). But supposing having given every indication that he is going to proceed with the protest he decides not to go through with it (he may have had a re-think and decided you were in the right after all) or he fails to satisfy one of the validity requirements and his protest is refused. Now a third yacht, who saw the collision, may lodge a protest against both of you because neither of you lodged a (valid) protest, and if the protest committee is satisfied that there was contact which was not minor and unavoidable, it will disqualify both of you. Alternatively, the protest committee may read in the other yacht's invalid protest that there was evidence of contact, and the committee itself initiate a hearing and decide at that hearing that there was contact and no valid protest, retirement, or penalty, and disqualify both yachts. Even if the other yacht's protest is valid, a protest committee is often sceptical of a yacht having had a collision, claiming she was in the right, and not herself lodging a protest. The best advice I can give on this point is this: if you have any incident in which your boat makes contact (any sort of contact) and you think you are in the right, and the other yacht does not retire or take a penalty, you should shout 'protest', and display a protest flag, and if you have any doubts that he did not retire or take a penalty in relation to that particular incident, lodge a written protest. You should do this whether the incident occurred in a club race or a world championship.

The other situation where you are effectively obliged to lodge a protest is when your yacht is forced by another yacht to make contact with a mark, and the infringing yacht does not retire or take a penalty. Even though your boat did not make contact with another yacht, if you want to sail on without taking the $360°$ penalty turn, the rules require you to lodge a valid protest. Failure to do so will mean you will be disqualified if there is a valid protest against you. If the protesting yacht is the yacht that didn't give you room, then he would be disqualified for not giving you room and you would be disqualified for hitting a mark and not lodging a valid protest.

So in summary, if there is an incident in which you feel you were in the right and another yacht was in the wrong, and the other yacht does not retire or take a penalty, and your yacht makes contact with another yacht or a mark, you should lodge a protest, whatever the event.

## When else should you protest?

Imagine in a world championship fleet race you are expecting to come in the top three overall; you are coming off the start line on starboard tack and you have to duck behind a boat on port tack. The port tacker is one of the other two. You genuinely had to bear away to avoid him. In this situation, you would obviously protest (shout 'protest' and display a protest flag). If the other yacht was a 'rabbit' (the rather innocuous term for a 'middle of the fleet' sailor) you wouldn't bother. Successful competitive sailors don't waste energy on protests if they don't think their overall position will be affected. Remember if there is no contact, there is no obligation to protest.

You see contact between two other yachts and neither protests or takes a penalty. Should you lodge a 'third yacht' protest against both of them? If they finish ahead of you and your protest succeeds they will both be disqualified and your result for that race will be enhanced by two places. You have to display a protest flag and hail your intention to protest, but you could be sneaky and pretend they were not in ear-shot at the time, and tell them later when it's too late for them to take a penalty or display a protest flag themselves. Personally I have never lodged a 'third yacht protest' and I dislike the rule that allows the procedure. I know plenty of competitors that do protest under these circumstances, even in club races. They are not wrong to do so. That's the way the game is described in the rule book. They justify their action by claiming that it is a 'no contact' sport and we must all do our bit towards keeping it that way, or that these two yachts have somehow 'infringed against the fleet' and deserve punishment. Personally I wouldn't feel happy about winning a championship by successfully protesting two yachts in this way.

You see a fellow competitor you think is infringing rule 54, shall we say pumping or rocking. Should you protest? If you do, how likely will your protest be upheld? Unless the protestee's evidence concurs with yours (unlikely unless he has misunderstood the limitations in rule 54) your evidence alone is unlikely to be sufficient to satisfy the protest committee that he has infringed rule 54, and your protest is likely to be dismissed. That is not to say you should not protest, because even if the protest is not upheld, the alleged infringement will get a good airing and the protestee will probably change the way he sails. One of the problems with protesting a yacht for infringing rule 54 is that to come up with sufficient evidence often means taking your attention from sailing your own boat, and many sailors are reluctant to do that. Protests alleging an infringement of rule 54 are rare at minor events. At championships, most protests alleging an infringement of rule 54, and certainly most successful protests, are initiated by representatives of a protest committee which accepts as one of its responsibilities the 'enforcement' of rule 54. However, whatever the level of event, if you see a yacht obviously infringing rule 54, and you think protesting will not damage your own performance, you should certainly protest.

## Insurance claims and damage

When your boat is damaged during an incident, and you think the skipper of the other yacht is responsible, you will want the owner or his insurance company to pay for the repairs.

By participating in a yacht race yachts thereby agree to be

governed by the yacht racing rules and to accept the penalties imposed by a protest committee (or an appeal authority if a decision goes to an appeal) and not to resort to any outside court or tribunal. [1]

[1] Fundamental rule B

The racing rules say nothing about who must pay for damage, though rule 76.1 invites national authorities to make a prescription to answer this question. It is unfortunate that most national authorities have not been able to provide a clear prescription. It certainly would not be practical or desirable for protest committees to make judgements about the value of damages; that is for the parties and their insurance companies and, as a last resort, courts of law to decide. However, as to who pays the damages, it is quite obvious that if there is a protest hearing, then it must be whoever the protest committee finds to be at fault. If there is no protest hearing, and a yacht retires voluntarily or accepts an alternative penalty, then although that does not in itself necessarily mean she has accepted that she infringed a rule, it would usually be difficult to come to any other conclusion.

A circuit appeals court in the United States recently made an important decision. '...when [yachts] voluntarily enter a yacht race for which published sailing instructions set out the conditions for participation, a private contract results between participants...'. Thus the rules (International Yacht Racing Rules, Sailing Instructions, Class rules etc.,) replace the International Collision Regulations for Preventing Collisions at Sea, and any other local collision regulations, provided that no other (non-racing) vessel is involved. The IYRU racing rules include a procedure (for a protest committee to conduct hearings, and usually an opportunity to appeal a decision) to determine fault when there is a dispute, of which the parties may avail themselves. Only the quantitative value of damages may be decided by a court (when not agreed by the parties). As to where the fault lies, if there is a protest hearing then fault is determined by the protest committee's decision.[2]

[2] United States Court of Appeals, First Circuit, 95-1426 *Juno* v *Endeavour*.

Many insurance policies contain what I consider to be an outrageous condition: that the policy holder is prohibited from admitting liability, and should he inadvertently do so, the policy will become invalid, and the insurance company will not pay the claim. So when a decent owner on port tack without a proper lookout runs into you when you are on starboard tack and damages your boat and wants to accept responsibility, you may find him reluctant to do so, or having accepted responsibility, denying it days later when he has been in contact with his insurance company.

### So here is my advice to you if there is damage (to either yacht) and you think it was not your fault.

If your boat is damaged by another yacht that was racing (or was intending to race and was sailing in the vicinity of the starting line or had been racing and had not left the vicinity of the course) and you believe the other yacht was to blame, there are some things you can do to improve the chances of the cost of repairs being met by the other yacht's owner or his insurance company.

The first thing to do is hail 'protest' and display a protest flag, irrespective of whether the other yacht indicates she is going to retire or take a penalty. Even if you see her take the penalty or actually withdraw from the race, nevertheless make the hail and display a red flag conspicuously as soon as you can. Continue to display the protest flag until the end of the race. (If the incident happens near the finish, then display the flag and draw the race committee's attention to it until the committee acknowledges seeing it.)

Prepare a written protest.

If you think the owner of the other yacht, let's say *Gay Abandon* will accept that his yacht infringed a rule, write the following words on the protest form; 'I accept that my yacht *Gay Abandon* sail number 1234 infringed racing rule 47 in the incident described in this protest. Signed ........... '. It would be unfair to ask him to sign that he takes responsibility for the cost of repair to the damage, as by doing so he may be invalidating his insurance policy. If he indicates that he will accept that he infringed a rule (perhaps by taking an alternative penalty immediately after the incident) but then, faced with being asked to sign a statement to that effect, changes his mind, then lodge the protest. The protest committee must hear the protest (assuming it's valid) unless he will accept that he 'acknowledges the infringement'. Whether or not he retired or took a penalty, and for what reason he retired, is irrelevant.[1]

[1] See rule 68.8

If your boat is damaged so badly that you have to retire immediately, or you have to attend to an injured crew member, hail immediately your intention to protest, and display the flag as soon as you can, if you can. If it is never possible to display the flag (you may have been too busy attending to an injury or saving the vessel), then when validity is being addressed by the protest committee, you must explain that you never had the 'opportunity' envisaged in rule 68.3(b).

When there is no valid protest from a yacht, the protest committee may itself initiate a hearing when it has 'reasonable grounds for believing that an infringement resulted in serious damage'[2], but it is not obliged to do so.

[2] Rule 70.2 (c)

What you are trying to achieve is a protest form describing the incident which has on it either the declaration by the other party that he acknowledges the infringement, or the finding of fact and decision by the protest committee that the other yacht infringed a rule. Such a protest form with the signed declaration or decision should mean that the other owner will become liable for full payment of the cost of your repairs. It is a powerful instrument, and in my experience it will almost invariably result in his bearing the full cost of repairs.

Furthermore, I recommend that should you decide to handle the case yourself rather than hand the protest form to your insurance company (you may need to deal directly with the other owner to preserve your 'no claims' bonus), you should deal with the other owner rather than his insurance company. After getting two or three estimates for repairs, write to him explaining the claim, and enclosing a copy of the estimates and a copy of the protest form with either his signed declaration or the committee's decision.

## International Regulations for Preventing Collisions at Sea ('IRPCAS' or 'Colregs')

If two yachts are racing, or intending to race and sailing in the vicinity of the starting line, or having finished or retired are within the vicinity of the course, then Part IV of the rules (the 'right-of-way rules') applies between them. It is irrelevant whether yachts are in the same race or different races or whether one or both has not yet started or whether the preparatory signal has been made by the race committee or whether either has finished.

However, if none of these criteria applies to either yacht, then Colregs apply to both yachts. Whether or not the preparatory signal or the starting signal has been made is irrelevant, what matters is where you are, and where the other yacht is, and whether either of you intends to race or has been racing.

The sailing instructions may prescribe that the Colregs apply in place of Part IV of the racing rules, and it is usual for them to do so from sunset when the race is expected to extend into the night; but when Part IV of the racing rules is in force, then the Colregs have no relevance whatever, unless of course a yacht that is not racing (or some other vessel) arrives on the scene!

Under the Colregs, when a give-way vessel on a collision course fails to take action and a collision becomes possible, a burden is placed on the right-of-way vessel to take action (if she is able to do so). As the vessels get closer, this burden increases. Thus, unless one vessel is unable to manoeuvre, it is almost impossible for two colliding vessels not to share (albeit unequally) the responsibility for any resulting damage.

## How to protest

Firstly you must inform the protestee. Usually this done simply by hailing 'protest' immediately after the incident.

Next you usually must display a protest flag conspicuously immediately after the incident.

When you come ashore you need to write the protest. As a minimum you must include the identity of the protestee, and sufficient details to identify the incident. At this stage it is worth recording some notes for your own reference (see 'preparing your case' below).

You must hand in the protest form to an appropriate official within a time limit, but if the time limit has expired and there is a legitimate reason why the protest is late, it may nevertheless be accepted.

You need to find out where and when the hearing will take place.

If you decide to bring witnesses you need to locate them and ask them to stand by when the hearing is scheduled.

Finally, you need to attend the hearing.

## Validity

For a protest to be heard it has to be valid; that is, certain requirements must be met. When a protest is not valid, the protest committee must refuse it; when it is valid, the protest committee must hear it. The protest committee has no discretion except that under certain circumstances it may allow it to be withdrawn, or, if a party acknowledges an infringement, not hear it. The usual requirements for a protest to be valid, are a hail of 'protest', a conspicuous and promptly displayed protest flag, and a written form describing the incident lodged within the time allowed for lodging protests. However, these validity requirements can be reduced in the sailing instructions (for example 'no protest flag is required'), and others added (such as the annoying and unnecessary requirement to inform the race committee vessel at the finishing line, or having to use a protest form supplied by the race committee).

## The hail

The first requirement is to hail an intention to protest. This seems simple enough. A loud shout of 'protest' will usually be sufficient. The hail doesn't commit you to anything; it is a claim that in your opinion the other yacht has infringed a rule and at that moment you intend to lodge a protest. You might change your mind. The most obvious reason for changing your mind is that he shouts back something like 'Sorry, I'll take a penalty' and proceeds to sail clear.

Remember, if you don't shout 'protest' immediately, you cannot lodge a protest. The hail doesn't have to heard for this validity requirement to be satisfied, but you have to be reasonable: hail more than once if the first hail is not acknowledged, and loud enough to be heard in the prevailing conditions.

What is the hail for? The racing rules don't give reasons, but it may be worth bearing in mind that there are two reasons for a hail. The hail can be a 'challenge' (so that the other yacht might decide to retire or take a penalty) and it 'marks the moment' so that the protestee will remember the occasion and be able to recall it when giving evidence. Whether or not either of these reasons are relevant to a particular case is neither here nor there; when the rules require a hail, then a hail must be made for the protest to be valid.

Often the protestor says he hailed and the protestee says he didn't hear the hail. Saying he didn't hear a hail is not the same as claiming the hail wasn't made, so when the evidence from the protestor is that the hail was made and the evidence from the protestee is that he didn't hear it, the committee will usually decide that the hail was made.

There are a few situations where a hail is not required. They are the same situations in which a protest flag is not required, so they are covered at the end of this next section on protest flags.

If you don't use the word 'protest' you must use words that make it clear that you intend to lodge a protest. Phrases like "Do your turns or else!", "Do a 720" and "See you in the jury room" will be ruled by some protest committees as not meeting the requirement. My recommendation is to use one word "protest" and if there is no apparent reaction, repeat it loudly. Remember that when the protest committee finds as a fact that no hail was made when it should have been, it has no discretion; it must rule the protest as invalid and refuse it. To emphasise the point, when a single-handed helmsman is knocked unconscious and cannot hail, he cannot protest. A flaw in the rules of course.

## The protest flag

In most cases, a yacht wanting to protest must display a protest flag, and failure to display a flag promptly, or conspicuously, or continuously would render a protest invalid. Generally, a flag is required when the protestor knows or could have known about the alleged infringement during a race.

The flag must be displayed conspicuously (so it can't be 1cm square, or displayed so low in the rigging that it can hardly be seen). It must be displayed at 'the first reasonable opportunity which is normally immediately after the incident'. The validity of many protests fail on this point. A delay for reasons of safety of the crew or vessel is permitted. A delay for tactical reasons is not. A delay because the flag can't be found or is stored in an awkward place is not acceptable. A short delay while the protestee responds to the hail of 'protest' and decides whether or not he will take a penalty is usually allowed.

When the first opportunity to display the flag occurs after finishing, it must still be displayed 'until acknowledged by the race committee'. If you have an incident very near the finishing line it is obviously worth prompting the race committee to acknowledge the display of your flag, which if the race committee is ashore might mean approaching an official as soon as possible after you come ashore.

The flag must be 'displayed until the yacht finishes or, when the first opportunity occurs after finishing, until acknowledged by the race committee'. So having displayed the flag conspicuously immediately after the incident, (which could be achieved by waving it), the protestor is required to continue displaying it until his yacht finishes. If it falls overboard, the requirement will not be met, and the protest is likely to be ruled as invalid.

The procedure of hailing and displaying a flag does not commit you to lodging a protest, it simply reserves your right to lodge a protest.

When you already have a flag displayed (from a previous incident) you don't need to display another, nor dip it or make any indication to it. The requirement to display a flag is automatically satisfied. To display a flag at the beginning of a race or before a race so as to avoid the necessity of displaying one in the event of a later decision to protest could be construed as infringing Fundamental Rule C (fair sailing), or a 'gross breach of good sportsmanship'.[1]

[1] Rule 75.1(a)

Some sailing instructions require a protestor to inform the race committee after finishing the sail number of the protestee, and failure to do so would render the protest invalid. Look for any special requirements in the sailing instructions. If you are involved in writing sailing instructions, please don't add to the already burdensome requirements in the rule book!

Many protests are in fact heard without some of these requirements having been met, but that's because the majority of protest committees are not aware of their obligation to satisfy themselves that a protest is valid before hearing it. When an astute (and often guilty) protestee forces the committee to address itself to the question of whether the protest is valid, the committee will have to make a decision on each validity question. If it hears a protest that it should rule as invalid and disqualifies the protestee, and the protestee had claimed all along that the protest was invalid, then an appeal would invariably succeed.

It's difficult to give detailed guidance on what constitutes 'conspicuous' or 'immediately' or 'the first reasonable opportunity'. The phrases speak for themselves, and protest committees will have differing ideas about each question; but decisions must be reasonable or risk being overturned on appeal. I will say that many protests are ruled as invalid when the hail is made fifteen seconds after the incident (the protestor probably waiting to see if the protestee is going to take a penalty), or when a protest flag appears after a minute.

Generally, yachtsmen don't like these stringent validity requirements which lead to many disputes remaining unsettled, and infringing yachts not penalised. Some protest committees take the view that if the protestee knew at the time of the incident that the protestor intended to lodge a protest, then the hail and the flag are irrelevant and should be unnecessary, but the rules do not at present support this view.

Some dinghy sailing clubs write in their sailing instructions that no flag is required, and report that everyone is happier at not having to get into complicated arguments about whether or not the flag requirements were met. A hail is then all that's needed. Very sensible.

There are some important exceptions to the 'protest flag' requirements.

Firstly, if you are sailing a yacht single handed, you may choose not to continue to display the flag till you finish, but should you take up this option you must take on another obligation: to 'have it acknowledged by the race committee when you finish'. If you sail single handed you may think it an attractive option not to have to find a way of displaying the flag between the time you first display it (immediately after the incident) and when you finish but many a protest has been ruled as invalid because the single handed protestor forgot to get the flag acknowledged at the finish.

Secondly, you don't need to display a flag if the incident happens other than 'during a race'. 'During a race' is not a defined term. The obvious interpretation is between the starting signal and the moment the last yacht finishes, but you'd be wise to display a flag if you want to protest about an incident that happens during the preparatory period when you are 'racing' according to the definition.

You don't need to display a flag if you have no knowledge of the facts justifying the protest until after you have finished or retired. For example, you see something on another yacht which is against the class rules, and realise she was sailing in that state during the last race.

You don't need to display a protest flag when you see two yachts make contact and neither takes a penalty or retires, and one does put up a flag and hail, and you assume she will lodge a protest but in fact fails to do so. You may then lodge a protest without having hailed or displayed a flag, but you may protest only under rule 33 (Contact between yachts racing).

## Preparing your case

There is nothing more frustrating than losing a protest when you know for sure you were in the right. As in most things in life, success depends largely on being properly prepared.

Before you ever get involved in a protest, you should prepare a page of important data about your boat. Draw up a table, with rows labelled 'Close-hauled smooth water', 'Close-hauled choppy water', 'Beam reaching smooth water', and so on. Each table should have columns headed 'Windspeed', 'Boatspeed' (in knots or feet/second or metres per second - whatever you are most used to), and 'Seconds to travel one boat length' - that's most important. When a protest is about an interaction between two or more yachts, extract from the table the relevant figures for the imminent protest hearing, and have them ready.

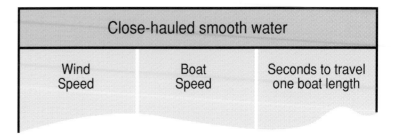

| Close-hauled smooth water | | |
| --- | --- | --- |
| Wind Speed | Boat Speed | Seconds to travel one boat length |

When you are about to lodge a protest, take a blank piece of paper and draw a sequence of diagrams. Start with the position of the boats before the incident and label the group '1'. Then draw the next set of boats when they have moved on a boat length or so, and label that group '2', and so on. Make sure that the sequence is logical; if one boat is moving faster than the other, make sure it moves relatively a little further each time. This process of thinking what happened, in slow motion, and without the pressures of being in the hearing, is very important. When you think you have worked it out, and corrected any anomalies, copy the sequence carefully onto the protest form.

Next identify the critical issues. On what fact will the result of the protest turn? Maybe it will be whether there was an overlap when the leading yacht became within two lengths of the mark. Which yacht's length is used? What does 'overlap' mean? There is bound to be conflicting evidence; when the committee are not satisfied one way or the other, is there an onus clause to which it will turn?

Make some notes to remind you in the hearing what facts you need to establish.

If you own a PC and have the computer programme 'RULEBOOK'[1], run through the incident as you remember it, then run through it as you think the protestee might claim it happened. Note all the statements which come up on the screen as a result of your answers (or print them out if you have access to a printer). Assuming that your answers result in your not infringing, enter what you think the protestee's answers will be. There will be just one or two that differ between the incident as you remember it and the incident as your opponent remembers it. For example, you are protesting against *Snatchit* for getting a late inside overlap at the mark, and taking room to which he was not entitled. It is obvious by comparing your version with his, that the critical issues will be: did Snatchit establish the overlap before you reached two lengths from the mark, and did

[1] The 'RULEBOOK' programme is for MS DOS. For details of the agent in your country, contact the publisher A1 Systems, PO Box 90496, Auckland Mail Centre, New Zealand, phone 64-9-418-1000, fax 64-9-377-3685.

Snatchit force you to give her room? The result of the protest will be determined by these two issues. Have that firmly in your mind.

Consider also the validity of the protest. Will the protestee make an issue of any of the validity criteria? Make notes about how you satisfied the hail and flag requirements. You probably will not need to refer to many of your notes, but writing them helps to clarify them in your mind.

Most of what is said in most hearings is totally irrelevant, in that it will not affect the outcome of the protest. Be aware of the issues that will count.

## Writing the protest

Unless the sailing instructions say otherwise, the protest must be in writing.

The written protest can be on any piece of paper but if standard protest forms are available, it is easier to use one.[1]

Many protestors write too much on the protest form. Prolific writers can miss the deadline for lodging protests, or can be embarrassed when they find in the hearing that what they wrote doesn't line up with the oral evidence presented at the hearing, or can confuse or bore the members of the protest committee. Perhaps the biggest disadvantage is the energy and effort expended in writing a long story and drawing complicated diagrams.

However, it is important to write legibly and clearly what happened and, when relevant, to draw a neat diagram depicting the sequence of events.

The minimum required by the rules is that the protest form 'identifies the nature of the incident'. When this requirement is not satisfied, the protest is invalid. The phrase 'port and starboard' under 'description of incident' with no diagram would not be sufficient to satisfy the rule.

The reason for the requirement to 'identify the incident' is so that the protestee can prepare a defence .

When the incident includes contact, you need to decide whether to disclose this fact in the protest form. If there is any chance that your protest may be ruled as invalid, it is best not to speak of 'contact' in the written protest, as the protest committee might disqualify both the parties.[2]

## Lodging the protest in time

Up to the point at which you 'lodge' a protest, you can decide not to go ahead with it. After you lodge it, other than in one of two rather unusual situations, you cannot withdraw it.

'Lodging' means handing it to a representative of the protest

[1] Sometimes there is a sailing instruction: 'A protest shall be written on a protest form available from the race office' in which case of course it has to be used. There is no justification for such a sailing instruction, but some organisers seem to delight in including as many obstacles as possible.

[2] Rule 70.2(b)(ii)

committee or race committee. Sailing instructions of major
championships often prescribe exactly where you must hand it in, in
other words, what constitutes 'lodging'.

One reason you might have for not lodging a protest is that even if it
is successful and the protestor is disqualified, the result won't affect
your race or series result (for example you finished the race ahead of
the yacht you are protesting). If there has been no contact, not to
proceed with the protest is perfectly acceptable. However, if you had
a collision, a third yacht might lodge a protest against both you and the
yacht with which you made contact, claiming you both infringed rule 33
which requires that where there is contact and neither yacht retires or
takes a penalty, one or both parties must lodge a valid protest.

If you finished the race, you must lodge your protest within the time
limit. If nothing has been prescribed in the sailing instructions, then
the time limit is 'two hours after the time that the last yacht finished'.
However, accepting a protest lodged after the time limit has expired
is within the power of the protest committee provided it 'has reason to
extend'. A typical reason would be that it took all yachts a long time to
sail back from the race course.

If you retired from the race, whether or not the retirement was
anything to do with the incident you're protesting about, then unless
there is a sailing instruction setting a time limit, it is up to the protest
committee to decide what is 'reasonable in the circumstances'. If the
race is a long one, the committee might think it reasonable that you
submit your protest earlier than the 'two hours after the last yacht
finishes'.

If you were disabled in the incident, forced to retire, and it took you
several hours to get back to the clubhouse, and you then lost no time
in lodging the protest, the committee must extend the time limit and
accept it. If you came in from the race, took a shower, went out to
dinner, and then lodged your protest, it is unlikely to be accepted,
and I'd go so far as to say that if you were the protestee, and the
committee accepted the protest which was late for no good reason,
you would be successful on appeal  in reversing the decision to
extend the protest time.

Ask for a photocopy of your own protest.

## Finding and preparing witnesses

The best witnesses are those who will be accepted as independent
by the protest committee, who saw the incident clearly and have the
same recollection as you do about what happened. Finding a good
witness from another yacht is often difficult and a member of your
own crew is often the only witness.

You don't have to have a witness. A single-handed sailor can win a
protest when there have been no witnesses (other than the two
parties), and a representative who decides to bring no witnesses can

win a protest when the other party brings several.

A bad witness at best wastes time and annoys the members of the protest committee, and at worst can act against the interests of the representative who brought him. I have seen countless examples of witnesses who have been useful to the 'opposing side'.

There is no limit to the number of witnesses you can call, but if you have many witnesses available, you should consider carefully who to call.

When asking a competitor to be a witness, you need to be sure he saw the incident in the same way you did, or at least in a way that supports your case. For example: your case revolves around whether or not you established an overlap in time, you approach a prospective witness before the hearing and ask him 'Do you think I had an overlap when Winatallcosts came within two lengths of the mark?' to which he replies 'Oh yes definitely, you had an overlap, I saw it all'. In the protest room when asked by the chairman to give his version of events, he places you with an overlap on the outside, or says you had an inside overlap but places the models showing no overlap. I've often seen this happen.

Worse is the friend who really saw nothing but is willing to be told what to say. When questioned he reveals a remarkable lack of recall about anything on which he was not briefed. The committee members are then inclined not to believe any of his evidence, and to suspect you of 'twisting the truth'.

I recommend that you ask a potential witness what he saw and if his version supports your case, consider asking him to be a witness. If it doesn't then don't ask him to be a witness. You could certainly give him a set of model boats or a few teaspoons and ask him to show you what he saw, but I recommend you don't tell him what to say. Ask him as many questions as you like but don't tell him anything.

In a technical protest (about measurement for example), you may bring an 'expert' as a witness, someone who did not necessarily see the 'incident' but can speak to support your case.

Occasionally, the person you ask to give be a witness refuses to attend the hearing, maybe because if you win your protest, he, or a friend or fellow national will lose a place. You cannot force him to give evidence. When the chairman asks if you have any witnesses the best thing to do is to say that there was a yacht who you feel could give useful evidence and you had approached the helmsman and asked him to be a witness but he had refused; and that you would be very pleased if the other party (the protestee if you are protesting) or the jury would call him as a witness. This may be unlikely, but it makes a point. Sometimes the person you approach and ask to be a witness won't because he's not prepared to give the time. In such a case he may be prepared to complete and sign a statement which you can present at the hearing. However, this is usually of limited value.

## Appearing before the committee

If you are protesting (rather than defending a protest), you are expected to make some effort to find out the time and place of the hearing. Failure to do so could result in the hearing going ahead without you. If there are several hearings and yours is not the first, you may be kept waiting for some time  (although a good jury secretary at a championship will repeatedly reschedule hearings to keep the waiting to a minimum). However, since there is no way of telling in advance how long a hearing will take, at least one set of parties has to be kept waiting.

As a party to the protest, you have a right to be present (as does the other party) during all of the taking of evidence, and you have the right to question anyone who gives evidence.

## Answering questions about validity

You will need to answer questions about when you hailed, or informed the protestee that you were going to lodge a protest, and about the flag, and if the protest was lodged outside the protest time why this was so.

After telling the committee about your hail and the flag, the protestee will sometimes claim he didn't hear the hail or see the flag. You may feel certain that in fact he did hear your hail because of the way he reacted, perhaps with an oral or visual response. No matter what you think of him, keep cool and say what you remember happening. If he denies hearing the hail and denies seeing the flag, when you know you hailed loud enough for him to hear, and you feel sure he saw the flag, don't get upset. Protest committees, especially those at major championships, are quite used to protestees questioning the protestor's evidence about validity, and if they suspect he is not being truthful, it will affect the credibility of the protestee's evidence when it comes to the situation itself. When the protest committee is satisfied with your evidence about validity it is likely to rule the protest as valid.

## Giving evidence

Firstly, some general advice! Always be honest, open and frank. Never set out to win a protest when you are sure you are in the wrong. If you're not sure who's in the right and who's in the wrong, give your evidence honestly and let the protest committee decide. If you lie in a protest hearing, this is what may happen:

You will lose the respect of your friends.
You will get a reputation, and even when you are telling the truth, you are unlikely to be believed.
The protest committee may initiate a 'rule 75' case, and you may be penalised very severely. Remember if you are penalised at all in a rule 75 hearing, the case will be referred to your national authority. It

will be like having a police record.

Remember, lying in a hearing is cheating. Don't even think about doing it. The penalties for cheating can be very severe. I have been involved as a judge in about thirty 'rule 75' hearings. Five were about lying in a hearing; all of which resulted in disqualification from the whole series, and of course being reported to the national authority.

## Opening statements

Once the committee has decided that the validity requirements have been satisfied, each party is invited to make an opening statement. If you are the protestor, even if you have described your version clearly in your protest form, you will still be expected to go through it orally. If the case is about an incident involving the yachts, you'll probably be given some model boats to push round. Don't talk too much; don't repeat yourself. Start by placing the models at some point before the incident and explain their relative positions, and what tack each was on, and where you were in relation to the nearest mark. If you are going to say that you were four boat-lengths from the mark, then put the models about four lengths from a mark; many people say four lengths and place them at two - then they run out of space to manoeuvre them.

After explaining the starting point, move the models on, say a boat length. If your boat was going faster than the other one, make sure you move it further than the other one. Move frame by frame at one or half lengths at a time until the moment of collision or infringement, and then explain what happened at that moment and why you think there was an infringement. Finally, say what happened after the incident. Unless the incident was very complicated, the opening statement should take no more than a few minutes.

If you are the protestee, then do the same thing. Move the boats frame by frame. At the frame when the protestor claims there was an infringement, explain why you think there wasn't.

## Questioning for clarification

After the protestor has given his opening statement, the chairman may invite the protestee to ask 'questions of clarification'. If you are the protestee, don't give your story at this stage, but if you don't understand something that the protestor has said, then ask a question to get the matter clarified.

## Witnesses

You will be invited to bring witnesses. You can bring as many as you like (though it usually unwise to bring more than one or two). The other party may bring any number of witnesses. The protest committee itself may call witnesses. A member of the protest committee may be a witness (indeed any of the members of the protest committee who have seen the incident should give evidence). The parties may question any of the witnesses. No-one can force a witness to attend a hearing or give evidence. Many protests are won without a witness being brought.

## Written evidence

Written evidence is of little value if the author does not attend the hearing to answer questions about his evidence. However, where a witness is unable to attend, a written statement can sometimes be worthwhile.

## Photographic evidence

In the vast majority of cases, photographic evidence is not a possibility, but even when it is, it's seldom of much use. A video recording can provide conclusive evidence about when things happened in the incident, but distances are very difficult to judge. But there have been cases determined on video evidence.

## Closing statements

At the end of all the giving of evidence from the parties and other witnesses, the two parties are invited to make a closing statement. You should take this opportunity to speak only of the relevant evidence and maybe draw the committee's attention to a rule or relevant case law. Don't take longer than half a minute.

## When you win a protest

It is an acceptable practice to offer to shake hands and not unusual to buy the man a pint of beer!

On the procedural front, you need to be aware that although it unlikely, he may apply for a re-opening or, if appeals have not been denied, he might appeal.

## When you lose a protest

When the protest committee decide your protest is invalid, it is 'refused'.

When the committee is not satisfied that the protestee infringed a rule, or is satisfied that the protestee did not infringe a rule, then your protest is said to be 'dismissed'.

When the committee is satisfied that you infringed a rule, then you will be penalised (by being disqualified from the race, unless the sailing instructions have provided for some other penalty).  Although this is rare, it does happen occasionally; A protests B, and A is disqualified.

Sometimes both yachts are found to have infringed, in which case the protest is 'upheld' but both yachts are disqualified.

Most usually though, a dismissed protest means no yacht is penalised. If the committee finds as a fact that there was contact (whether or not it was 'minor and unavoidable'), then there must have been an infringement, and the committee must end up penalising at least one yacht.

When your protest is refused or dismissed, you need to decide whether or not to appeal, and whether or not to apply for a re-opening. If the protest committee is an international jury, then the decision is not open to appeal. If there is no international jury and the decision is open to appeal, but the facts found are reasonable (given the evidence presented to the committee) and you agree that the decision is correct given those facts, then an appeal would not succeed. If you are unhappy with the procedure, unless it was prejudicial an appeal will not succeed. A re-opening request will be granted only if you can either satisfy the committee it may have made an error, or you can come up with some relevant evidence which was not available at the time of the hearing.

## Defending a protest

### When to retire or take a penalty, when to 'counter protest'

Usually the first you know of a protest against you is immediately after an incident during a race when the protestor hails 'protest'. Then you have to make a decision.

If you know you have infringed a rule, and the '720 Turns Penalty' system is in force, immediately begin to sail clear of other yachts and, when clear, do your turns. It is polite to tell the would-be protestor that that is what you are going to do; 'OK I'll take a penalty'. If the 'Scoring Penalty' system is in force immediately display Code flag 'I'. If no penalty system is in force, retire from the race.

If you are not sure whether or not you infringed and there is a penalty system in force, you have to decide whether or not it is prudent to accept a penalty. You must think of the effect taking a penalty will have on your position in the series. You might decide it would be better to lose a little distance by taking a 720 turn penalty than risk disqualification in a hearing. If there is no alternative penalty in force, it is best to carry on in the hope that the other yacht will not go through with the protest, or if he does, that you will be exonerated.

If you are sure you didn't infringe a rule, then obviously you sail on.

If you think the other yacht infringed you should hail 'protest' and display a protest flag. This is a 'counter protest'.

You may take a penalty (if a penalty system is in force) or retire, and protest too. You need to hail 'protest' immediately, and display your protest flag, before you take the penalty.

### Questioning validity

When there is a protest and a counter protest (about the same incident), then provided at least one of the protests is valid, the hearing will proceed. There is no point in questioning the validity of the other yacht's protest.

If there is a protest against you, and you believe you have not infringed, but you do not believe the other yacht infringed either, you might believe he has not fulfilled the requirements for his protest to be valid. Did he hail 'protest'? When did his flag go up, and if after finishing did the race committee acknowledge the flag? Was his protest lodged in time. If you genuinely believe the requirements have not been met, you should question them, but remember that if the committee are going to be satisfied (from his evidence) that the validity requirements were met, it will not impress the committee that you were so keen to establish that the protest was not valid.

If there is a protest against you, you are entitled to study a copy before the hearing. Ensure you have a copy and make the same preparation as you would if you were protesting (including finding witnesses). Draw the sequence of events on a piece of plain paper to clarify in your mind what happened, so that when you give evidence it will be clear and logical. Know in advance what the critical issues will be.

As 'protestee' you will give your evidence last, and you will be given the opportunity to 'sum up' last.

See the section above on 'Preparing your case'.

# 6
# THE REDRESS HEARING

# 6 THE REDRESS HEARING

A redress hearing investigates whether a yacht's finishing position has been prejudiced by any one of several specific causes. A successful request will result in the protest committee making a decision 'as equitable as possible to all yachts concerned'. This usually means awarding to the requesting yacht 'redress' in the form of points equivalent to some artificial finishing position.

Most requests for redress claim that the race committee has done something wrong. You may also get redress when your yacht is damaged by a give-way yacht, but your yacht must be physically damaged (or the crew injured), not just delayed, for example by a capsize. Other legitimate reasons for requesting redress are being delayed by helping a person or yacht in distress, and your position being prejudiced by a yacht found guilty of unfair sailing.

As with a protest hearing, it is a good idea to sit down before the hearing and write some notes. Write how your request meets the requirements and what redress you think might be appropriate.

## Initiation

A redress hearing can be initiated in two ways. The race committee or protest committee can itself initiate a hearing when it believes the right conditions exist. For example, the race committee lifts a mark when there are still five boats left to round it, throwing them into confusion, and giving them no chance to catch the rest of the fleet, or even to sail the course. Realising its mistake and anxious that redress be awarded to the prejudiced yachts, the race committee initiates a redress hearing.

More commonly, a request for redress comes from an aggrieved yacht (or several yachts). Certain criteria have to be satisfied for a request to be valid (and, therefore, a hearing to proceed), and other criteria have to be satisfied for the request to be upheld (and, therefore, redress to be granted).

## Validity (for a hearing to proceed)

The request must be in writing and include the nature of the incident. It must be lodged within the time limit for lodging protests (two hours after the last yacht finishes unless the sailing instructions prescribe some other limit). However, the protest committee may accept a request after this time if there is a reason to do so.

When the cause for the request has happened after the race, or you have been unavoidably delayed returning from the race, for example by being seriously damaged in a collision, you should lodge the request as soon as you can. As no hail or flag is required, a request is rarely refused on the grounds that it is invalid.[1]

[1] A protest flag is required when the Match Racing Appendix is in force.

## Validity (for a request to be successful)

A hearing is usually granted, but to be awarded redress you have to establish several things.

Firstly, your finishing place in the race or series has to have been materially prejudiced through no fault of your own. If you won the series, your position can't have been prejudiced.

The prejudice must have been caused by one of the following.

* The race committee or the protest committee acted improperly (or improperly failed to act).

* You rendered assistance to a person or yacht in peril (as you are required to do by Fundamental Rule A).

* Your yacht was physically damaged by another vessel that was required to keep clear (the 'other vessel' might be another yacht which was racing and required to keep clear by the racing rules, or a yacht or some other vessel required to keep clear by the International Regulations for Preventing Collisions at Sea or by any other applicable regulations or laws).

* Your yacht was prejudiced by a yacht which infringed fundamental rule C (fair sailing) and which was then penalised under rule 75. This covers the rare case where, for example, *Winatallcosts* intentionally starts prematurely in the last race of a series with a discard, and interferes with her closest rival to protect her series position. *Winatallcosts* is found at a Rule 75 hearing to have infringed Fundamental Rule C, and is penalised by being disqualified from the whole series. The other yacht may be awarded redress.

## The hearing

As in a protest hearing, you appear as the representative of the yacht seeking redress. If you are claiming that an action by the protest committee itself has prejudiced your position, then you will appear alone; there will be no independent committee to investigate your case. If you are claiming that an action by the race committee prejudiced your position, then there will be someone to represent the race committee. If you are one of several yachts requesting redress about the same matter, you will probably all appear together at one hearing.

In the first part of the hearing, the committee may address whether your request is valid. The only question that might cause the request to be invalid is whether the request was received in time. If it was lodged after the closing time for the receipt of protests, the committee will need to be satisfied that it was lodged in reasonable time after you could have become aware of the problem. For example if you see in the results that you are scored as 10th whereas you know you came 5th, how long had the results been posted before you noticed the error? Did you make a reasonable attempt to see the results?

Next, you will be invited to explain your case. Bear in mind that you have to satisfy the committee on the following points; if you don't they cannot give you redress.

Firstly, your position in a race or series must have been prejudiced. If you won the race or series, your finishing position can't have been prejudiced. Suppose you come fifth in a race, and you had noticed that the race committee had been displaying the wrong code flag as the warning signal at the start. No one noticed, and no one was affected. No one can have been prejudiced and so no one can get redress. The race committee can, without sanction, infringe any of the rules governing its management of races provided that it doesn't prejudice any yacht's finishing position.

On the other hand, you would have a legitimate claim if your start was spoiled by the race committee moving the outer distance mark thirty seconds before the starting signal.

The next thing you will need to establish is that the prejudice was 'through no fault of your own'. Many requests come unstuck here. For example a sailing instruction requires all yachts to stay outside a 'box' before their preparatory signal, and gives the power to the race committee to disqualify without a hearing. Lots of yachts in your race ignore the instruction. Some, including you, are disqualified. You seek redress. You claim that you didn't get in anyone's way, and lots of others infringed the sailing instruction and were not penalised. It was unfair. The sailing instruction is new. You weren't made aware of it. And so on. You won't get anywhere with a request for redress. You were at fault. You infringed the sailing instruction.

Next it must have been for one of the permitted causes: for example, an improper action or omission by the race committee. 'Improper' doesn't necessarily mean that a rule has been infringed by the race committee. Rule 5.3(a) says the race committee can postpone a start for any reason, but if a start is postponed so that the race officer's son, having arrived late, can get to the starting area in time for the start, when everyone else is ready to start at the published time, then this would be improper, even though there is no rule infringed.

You have the right to call any number of witnesses, as does the race committee if its conduct is in question. The protest committee may call witnesses. The witnesses may be questioned.

Use your notes to sum up your case, saying how you have met the requirements for a valid claim for redress and perhaps suggesting an equitable solution.

## The decision

When the protest committee is satisfied that your finishing position was prejudiced, and that it was through no fault of your own, and that it was caused by one of the permitted reasons, then it must 'make a decision as equitable as possible to all yachts concerned'. It would be impossible to do this without knowing the probable consequences of making some particular arrangement, and rule 74.2(b) requires the protest committee to take appropriate evidence before making its decision as to what will be the most equitable arrangement. This usually means taking evidence from yachts that will be affected, even indirectly, by the redress given. Typically the leading yachts are asked to give their opinions.

Rarely is the most equitable arrangement to cancel a race. Even with a complex redress hearing where perhaps, because of an error of a race committee, half the fleet sailed one course and half sailed another, a better solution can often be found. For example allocating two first positions, two seconds, and so on. As a general rule, if yachts have, or even one yacht has, completed the course and finished and done everything required of them, then a good protest committee will be reluctant to take away their results.

Sometimes the most equitable arrangement is to give no redress and to simply let the results stand.

Provided that the right to appeal has not been legitimately denied, a decision not to hear a request for redress, or that the request does not meet the requirements, or the extent to which redress given is equitable, are all open to appeal.

# 7
# REQUESTING A HEARING

# 7 REQUESTING A HEARING

The race committee is permitted to penalise a yacht without a hearing only under certain specific circumstances. When a yacht fails to start or finish, the race committee may score her as DNS ('did not start'), or DNF ('did not finish'), irrespective of what position she was in when she crossed the finishing line. You may unknowingly cross the starting line a few seconds early and discover you have not been awarded a finishing position only when you see the results published on the notice board.

Some dinghy championship organisers include a sailing instruction to allow the protest committee to penalise a yacht without a hearing when a committee member sees what he believes to be an infringement of rule 54 (Propulsion).

However, in all cases where a yacht is penalised without a hearing, the yacht has the right to a hearing. You need simply to ask and it shall be given.

Sometimes a race committee will penalise a yacht without a hearing when it has no right to do so, but there is no reason to get upset; if the committee will give you a hearing upon request, then there is no prejudice. For example the race committee believes you sailed the wrong course (even though you crossed the finishing line correctly) and scores you as DNF (did not finish). The race committee had no right to disqualify you without a hearing but if you don't agree that you sailed the wrong course, you can ask for a hearing. If you accept that you sailed the wrong course, there's not really much point in asking for the hearing just to make the point that the committee shouldn't have penalised you without a hearing. (The correct procedure, by the way, when the race committee believes you sailed the wrong course, is to suggest you retire, and if you don't, initiate a hearing.)

When a yacht requests a hearing, if there is a protest committee appointed it will conduct the hearing. If no protest committee has been appointed, then the race committee itself may hear the case, but it is more usual (and more satisfactory) for the race committee to appoint a sub-committee to hear the case.

## Premature starter

A 'premature starter' is a yacht that crosses the starting line to start before her starting signal. Strictly speaking a premature starter doesn't actually start, since according to the definition a yacht starts only when she first crosses the start line after her starting signal. However, 'premature starter' is an oft used and convenient term for a yacht which is not wholly on the pre-course side of the starting line at the moment of the starting signal.

A premature starter is required to start. If you cross the starting line early, you must go back behind the line and start in accordance with the definition. You don't have to do it immediately or even as soon as you are aware (if you ever are aware) but if you are aware you were a premature starter, and you are able to return (there is room for you to turn back), and you sail on and interfere with another yacht (perhaps your closest rival), then you could be penalised under rule 75 for unsportsmanlike behaviour.

At some major championships, there is a sailing instruction requiring premature starters to retire (e.g. a 'black flag' rule).

When a yacht fails to start, the race committee will score her as DNS (did not start) or PMS (premature starter). If you find after the race that you have been scored as DNS or PMS and believe the committee was wrong, you are entitled to a hearing. You simply have to submit a request that you be given a hearing.

Let's take the case where the race committee has scored you as a premature starter and you believe you were behind the line at the starting signal. At the hearing you will need to satisfy the protest committee that the race committee made an error. If you can satisfy the protest committee that the error was an error of fact, for example that the race committee wrote down your sail number when in fact it was another yacht perhaps with a similar sail number that was over the line, then you will of course be reinstated. But if your claim is that the error was an error of judgement, you are most unlikely to succeed.

Next let's take the case where you accept that you were a premature starter but you claim that you did in fact return to the pre-start side and start correctly. If the race committee accepts that you returned but claims your boat did not get wholly across to the pre-start side, then that is a matter of judgement and unless you have conclusive evidence (such as a video taken from the right angle), the protest committee will accept the race committee's judgement rather than yours. However, if your claim is that you returned properly, and the race committee can offer no evidence as to whether or not you returned, then the protest committee will be inclined to accept your evidence that you did in fact return properly. When you claim you returned and the race committee is adamant you didn't return (rather than accepting you

returned but that you had not returned wholly to the pre-course side of the line), then the protest committee will assess the evidence from you and the race committee without bias, as it is not judgement which is being questioned.

To summarise, where there is a judgmental question being considered, the protest committee will need conclusive evidence from a yacht before it will overturn the decision of the race committee.

## Finishing Error

If you 'fail to finish according to the definition', the race committee may score you as DNF (did not finish) without a hearing. The most obvious example is when you are never seen to get near the finishing line. The only other situation is when you cross the line in the wrong direction (i.e. not 'from the direction of the last mark'). By the way, to 'cross the line', you need to get any part of your boat or crew or equipment in its normal position to cut the line; after that you can clear the line in any direction.

If you believe you have finished correctly but been scored as 'DNF', at a small event you could have a word with the race officer, and if he doesn't give you a satisfactory answer, only then submit a written request for a hearing. At a championship, it's best to submit a written request as soon as you are aware of the error (usually when you see the provisional results list). You may have finished in a bunch of boats and been missed, in which case the race committee is usually happy to insert you into the results without the necessity for a hearing.

## Rule 54 (Propulsion)

Sailing instructions sometimes include a clause[1] to permit a protest committee to disqualify a yacht without a hearing when one or more of its members sees an infringement of rule 54 (i.e. illegal propulsion, such as pumping or rocking). Such a procedure is fairly common at major dinghy championships. Some competitors don't like the system, but remember if ever you are unhappy about being disqualified without a hearing you can have a hearing simply by asking for one. Most competitors disqualified in this way do not bother to ask for a hearing because they think there is no chance of the decision to disqualify them being reversed. They are usually right.

However, if you are disqualified and believe you did not infringe the rule, you should most definitely ask for a hearing. The protest committee must present the evidence that led to your disqualification. Now you must make a decision; do you believe that you were doing what they said you were doing but that it didn't infringe the rule? Or do you accept that what the witnesses describe infringes the rule, but you were not doing what they say you were doing? Be focused on which standpoint you are going to argue. If you are successful (and it does happen) the protest committee will overturn its original decision.

[1] See rule 70.1(b).

9907
BANANE
GUADELOUP
O'NEILL
HOBIE CAT 16 WORLDS
GUADELOUPE

# 8
# RE-OPENING
# A HEARING

# 8 RE-OPENING A HEARING

You can apply to have any hearing (for example a protest hearing or a redress hearing, or hearing to address a starting or finishing infringement) to be re-opened, but before the protest committee can re-open the hearing a criterion has to be satisfied. If the criterion is satisfied, the protest committee must re-open the hearing,[1] and if the criterion is not satisfied then the protest committee must not re-open the hearing.

The protest committee may want to re-open a hearing without having received a request from a party to the original hearing, but the criterion must be satisfied before it may re-open. A good protest committee, if it realises it has, for example, disqualified the wrong yacht in a protest hearing, will not sit tight and hope the aggrieved party won't complain or is unaware of the procedure for applying for a re-opening, but will take the initiative and re-open without a request.

## Validity

One of the following criteria must be satisfied:

- The protest committee decides it may have made a significant error. A 'significant error' would be something like disqualifying the wrong yacht. An insignificant error might be finding that a yacht had infringed one rule when, on second thoughts, it was decided she had infringed another.

- Material new evidence becomes available within a reasonable time. 'New' means that it was not available at the time of the original hearing. 'Material' means there is a realistic possibility it will bring about a change to the original decision.

When appeals are permitted and an appeal is lodged, a national authority may direct a protest committee to re-open a hearing.

## The procedure

When the protest committee itself decides to re-open a hearing, the procedure is straightforward. Having decided one of the above criteria has been satisfied, it informs the parties (all of them) of a date and place for the re-opened hearing to take place.

When a party requests a re-opening, the protest committee must be satisfied that the criterion has been met before a hearing can be re-opened. The request must be lodged before 1800 on the day following the decision, but the committee may extend this deadline. It is reasonable for the protest committee to expect the applicant to make the request in writing and to explain in the request how the criterion has been satisfied, but usually an audience with the protest committee is the only way to hear the evidence necessary for the committee to decide whether the criterion has been met, if only to be seen to address the request properly and to explain why the criterion has to be satisfied.

As a judge, my own preferred procedure on receipt of a written request from a party to re-open, even if the request seems as though it does not fulfil the requirements, is to invite the parties (that is, the party making the request, and the other party (or parties) to the original hearing) to an audience with the protest committee. The chairman explains that this is not a re-opened hearing, but simply an opportunity for the requester to satisfy the protest committee that the requirements have been met, and to explain that unless they are met, the protest committee has no power to re-open.

The requester then states his case. He might show some evidence he claims to be both new and material. The other party is invited to comment; he might want to argue that the evidence is not new, or not material, or that there has been no 'significant error'.

Unless it is clear the requirements have or haven't been met, the parties are asked to withdraw, and the committee makes its decision as to whether the requirement has been met in which case the hearing will be re-opened, or has not been met in which case the hearing will not be re-opened.

The decision by the protest committee to re-open or not to re-open may be appealed (unless appeals have been denied).

When there is doubt as to whether or not the validity requirements have been met, and the competitor is convinced he has met the requirement, my own opinion is that the committee should re-open the hearing. This allows a competitor the chance to argue his case but does not commit the committee to reverse its original decision.

## The re-opened hearing

If after hearing a party's submission, and deciding that the criterion has been met and that the hearing will, therefore, be re-opened, the chairman might ask whether the parties are prepared to proceed immediately. If any of the parties are not present when the committee makes its decision to re-open, then they have to be informed in writing of the time and place of the re-opened hearing.

A majority of the members of the protest committee for the re-opened hearing shall, when possible, be members of the original

protest committee. In practice the membership of the committee is usually identical. A party certainly has no right to demand the re-opened hearing is heard by a new group.

## When to ask for a hearing to be re-opened

It is totally inappropriate to use the re-opening procedure to have a last ditch attempt to avoid being penalised after a hearing. Unless your re-opening request satisfies one of the two requirements to be met before a hearing can be re-opened, then you would be wasting your time and energy, to say nothing of annoying the protest committee.

However, when you believe that you have a legitimate claim for a re-opening, you should not hesitate to apply. You should write a letter to the protest committee which heard your original case. You could use a protest form if one is available, though many of the prompts will be irrelevant.

You need to identify the hearing which you are applying to re-open, and you must say why you think that one of the two reasons apply.

An experienced protest committee will usually give you an audience with the committee to give you a chance to expand on, or justify, your reasons.

Only you need to be present at this audience (it is not a hearing), though a protest committee might invite the other party or parties to attend. You may be asked to withdraw while the committee decides whether or not the requirements for re-opening have been met.

If you are advised that the hearing will not be re-opened and you feel that the requirements for re-opening have been met, you may appeal the committee's decision not to re-open (provided appeals are allowed, as they usually are).

# 9
# THE RULE 75
# HEARING

# 9 THE RULE 75 HEARING

A rule 75 hearing is rare. It investigates whether a person (not a yacht) is guilty of 'a gross infringement of the rules' or 'a gross breach of good manners' or 'a gross breach of sportsmanship'.

## Initiation

Oddly, there is no rule explicitly requiring a person to avoid 'grossly infringing the rules' or to 'behave in a good-mannered way', or to 'be a good sportsman', and there is no facility for a person to protest another person for an offence of this nature. However, if your own ideas about morality don't stop you cheating or behaving badly, the severe penalties that can be imposed in a rule 75 hearing certainly should! Only the protest committee can initiate a hearing, but it often acts after receiving a report from a competitor, or from hearing evidence of a gross infringement or a breach during a protest hearing. A rule 75 hearing can be initiated at any level of event; if a misdemeanour is to be investigated at a sailing club, a protest committee often has to be appointed specifically to hear the case.

## The 'infringement'

Rule 75 is worded broadly and allows the protest committee (and that includes the race committee acting as a protest committee when no protest committee has been appointed) to initiate a hearing for any one of a wide range of offences. Here are some examples.

- The most common is behaviour which could best be described as 'bringing the sport into disrepute'.

- Losing one's temper and using threatening behaviour, ramming another boat, offensive verbal abuse (to fellow sailors or officials), physical abuse.

- Bad language that offends.

- Cheating during the race to get a better result, such as leaving out a mark to gain some places.

- Lying in a hearing.

- Premeditated cheating. An example is building hidden weights into a hull, or centreboard, or building equipment to pump water ballast to the windward side of a keelboat.

## The non-infringement

Protest committees (and class associations and other official bodies) can sometimes get excited about what they think is cheating which is in fact nothing more than an attempt by a competitor to go to the limit of a rule. I can recall a case where a sailor in a dinghy class having studied the class rules was of the opinion that to alter the height position of the forestay attachment on the mast was not prohibited. He made the change in the hope that by raising the jib luff the boat would go faster. Since no one else had made this change, some class officials were convinced this was cheating and the offender should be the subject of a rule 75 hearing and drummed out of the class. In the event, common-sense prevailed and a simple measurement protest was initiated. The protest committee referred the case to the class measurement committee[1] who ruled the alteration was illegal, and put in hand the re-wording of a not-altogether clear class rule. A rule 75 hearing would have been quite inappropriate.

[1] When a protest committee is not sure about the interpretation of a class rule, the rules require that it refer the matter to 'an authority qualified to resolve such questions'.

Competitors who are keen to win in any sport will play every aspect of the game to the limit of the rules. The rules, after all, are there to describe the limits of the game.

## The hearing

The procedure is much the same as any other hearing. You get the 'accusation' in writing and are given a time and place for the hearing. You may apply for an adjournment if you are not ready to proceed. You appear alone before the committee[2] (there is no 'protestor'). The protest committee presents its case. You respond. The protest committee may call witnesses. You may call witnesses. You may question any of the witnesses. You may summarise your defence. The committee sits in private to make its decision. You appear before the committee to hear the result.

[2] If you want a legal advisor to attend, a wise protest committee will permit you to do so.

## When you are the subject of a 'Rule 75 hearing'

If you are informed that there is a hearing against you, firstly ensure you have a written copy of the allegations. If you are not happy to proceed at the time the hearing is called, then ask for time to consider your position.

Read the allegations carefully, and consider whether they are true.

Don't complicate and compound the situation; be polite and courteous to the officials involved.

You will appear alone before the committee. There is no 'protestor' though there might be a witness who initiated the report which brought about the hearing.

Ask yourself how guilty you feel. Was it a premeditated plan to gain an advantage knowing at the time it was illegal or unfair? Or was it a 'spur-of-the-moment action' which you now regret?

If the allegations are substantially true, the best course of action is to say so and explain why you did what you did. It could be that you have a short temper and something caused you to lose it. Explain what the something was. Maybe you were drunk and had lost your ability to act with propriety. If you are sorry for what you did, say so to the committee. Defending the accusations when they are substantially true often leads to a heavy penalty. A sincere apology often leads to a light penalty.

Rarely does a competitor who acted on the spur of the moment and is genuinely sorry get a big penalty, and often no penalty is imposed (and, therefore, his national authority is not informed).

## The penalty

When the committee is satisfied that one of the three clauses in rule 75 is applicable, it has the power to give a penalty within a wide range of possibilities from a warning to disqualification of the entire series. It cannot extend a disqualification to a period outside its jurisdiction (so if it was an international jury at a championship, the maximum penalty it could impose would be disqualification from the championship). Having imposed a penalty the protest committee must make a report to the national authority that had jurisdiction over the event and, if it's different, to the national authority of the person penalised.

Each national authority may impose a ban, preventing the offender (whatever country he comes from) from competing in events in its jurisdiction, and can suspend IYRU eligibility of its own nationals, preventing them from competing anywhere in the world in Olympic, World and Continental championships.

## Coaches and other support personnel

It is sometimes difficult for race organisers to find ways to control the behaviour of the small minority of coaches and other support personnel who at major championships ignore rules to keep them from the racing area or communicate with competitors during a race. I see nothing wrong with a sailing instruction that prescribes limitations on the behaviour of support personnel and when such rules are infringed the fact that penalties will be imposed on the competitors that they support. So if you are sailing in a major event and you have a coach, make sure he is aware of what might happen to *your* result if *he* infringes the rules.

# 10
# APPEALS

# 10  APPEALS

An appeal is a claim that a protest committee has made an error and should be directed to change its decision. Most appeals come from a yacht that was a 'party to the protest' (usually the protestee, but sometimes the protestor) that has been penalised after a hearing, or from a yacht claiming she has not been given redress to which she believes she is due, or that a protest committee should have opened a hearing but didn't.

An appeal is made to the national authority that had jurisdiction over the event. The USA, Canada and Australia have state appeals authorities. A deposit is usually required. You may have to wait several months for the result of an appeal.

The appeal authority can uphold your appeal and direct the race committee to reinstate you or give you redress. It might also decide to penalise another yacht. It might uphold your appeal to the extent that it directs the protest committee to re-hear the case (or to hear the case if the appeal is against a decision not to hear a case).

At some events there is no right to appeal.

## 'No appeal status'
At some events, decisions by the protest committee are not open to appeal. You cannot appeal when appeals have been legitimately denied.

- The right to appeal may be denied when the competition is a 'knock-out' event, where it is essential to determine promptly the results of races that enable yachts to qualify for the next round. National authorities often prescribe that their permission is required and usually do allow appeals in the final round. The organising authority must inform you of this in the notice of race and the sailing instructions.

- At large international championships, an 'international jury' is usually appointed. You cannot appeal against a decision of an international jury that is acting within its terms of reference. (The jury's terms of reference are in Appendix A5 of the racing rules, and may be varied in the notice of race and/or sailing instructions.) If you believe that the jury was acting outside its terms of reference, then you may appeal to the national authority that had jurisdiction over the event (which usually means in whose waters the event was held). The most usual example of an international jury acting outside its jurisdiction is when the membership requirement of 'minimum of five + a majority of International Judges + nationality spread' is not satisfied (these requirements are prescribed in Appendix A5 of the racing rules).

- You can't appeal when a national authority prescribes that there will be no appeals for an event open only to entrants under its own jurisdiction. This is unusual.

In all other cases, (which is 99.99% of events), any decision by a protest committee may be appealed.

## Who can appeal

You can appeal only if you are a party to a hearing (if you're not you'll have your appeal 'refused'). 'Parties' are the protestor and protestee, any other yacht penalised in a hearing, a yacht that has requested redress, and a competitor who is penalised under rule 75. If you've had a protest refused or ignored, or a request for a hearing or a re-hearing refused or ignored you may appeal.

The race committee may appeal against a decision of a jury[1] when its conduct is the subject of a redress hearing.

[1] A jury is a protest committee which is not an international jury but is independent of the race committee. A jury is appointed by the organising authority, typically at championships.

A protest committee may itself refer a case if it is not sure about the correctness of its decision. This is called a referral, but it's really no different to an appeal in that the appeal authority can overturn the protest committee's decision.

## What you can appeal about

You can appeal against most decisions and procedural errors, but you cannot appeal the facts found by the protest committee. This is a very important point and the cause of disappointment for many appellants.[2] It is not within the authority of the appeal body to assess the value of evidence and determine whether the protest committee came up with the best 'facts found'. The protest committee alone has that function, and it can put what weight it likes on various pieces of testimony.

[2] If the facts found by the protest committee are at complete variance with the evidence, or to put it another way, if the facts found are totally nonsensical given the total evidence presented, then most appeals authorities will consider the case, and may direct the protest committee to explain their decision, or direct it to re-hear the case, possibly with a new committee.

Appeals against procedural errors will succeed only if it can be shown that the errors were prejudicial.

At a guess, one third of appeals fail because they seek to overturn 'facts found'. About a third of the remainder are upheld. More than a third of all appeals relate to errors of race and protest committees.

Here are some typical examples of appeals which might succeed.

- A protest is lodged against you and the committee decide it is valid and hear the protest. You are penalised at the hearing. You believe you should not have been penalised because the committee has interpreted the rules incorrectly.

- A protest is lodged against you and the committee decide it is valid and hear the protest, but you believe it is not valid and should not have been heard. You express your view to the protest committee at the commencement of the hearing that the protest is invalid. You are penalised at the hearing. You appeal against the protest committee's decision to hear the protest.

- You lodge a protest and the committee hear it but do not uphold it (that is, the committee does not penalise the protestee). You believe the committee has interpreted the rules incorrectly.

- You lodge a protest and the committee decide your protest was invalid or simply don't address whether or not it was valid. You appeal against its decision to find the protest invalid, or the fact that the validity was not addressed, and that there was no hearing.

- You request redress and your request is refused, or you are given redress but you think the committee's decision was not 'as equitable as possible to all yachts concerned'.

Here are some examples of where an appeal will fail or be refused.

- At the protest hearing you claimed you established an overlap in proper time. You brought six witnesses to give evidence to that effect. The other party said there was no overlap and brought no witnesses. Yet the protest committee found as a fact that there was no overlap. You appealed the decision to find as a fact that there was no overlap. Included with your appeal papers were written statements from all the witnesses. How could the protestee committee believe the protestee? You are appealing against the facts found by the protest committee. The appeal will be dismissed.

- You were a witness for a protestor and to your surprise the protest was not upheld. Had it been upheld your position in the race would have been enhanced by one place. You have no right to appeal because you were not a party to the protest. The appeal will be refused..

- Another yacht requests redress and the request is upheld. The decision is to give several yachts (not just the yacht that requested redress) artificial finishing positions, and this adversely effects your position. You have no right to appeal because you were not a party to the hearing. The appeal will be refused. You could request redress claiming that the action of the protest committee has prejudiced your position, and appeal against the decision taken at that hearing.

## How to lodge an appeal

Within fifteen days of receiving the protest committee's written decision, you need to lodge the appeal with the national authority which had jurisdiction over the event.

In the USA an appeal must be lodged with a District Appeal Committee, and in Australia to the State Association. In Canada an appeal must be lodged to the relevant Provincial Appeal Committee. In the UK, an appeal is lodged with the relevant organising authority, which assembles the documents and submits the appeal to the Royal Yachting Association. When an organising authority is tardy or uncooperative, the appellant can ask the RYA to chase them.

Because many countries' national authorities prescribe variations to the standard procedure in the rule book, you will need to refer to the prescriptions to rule 78.

NED
4444
NED
4444
GER 4334
4334
M 36
OMEN
THOMAS I PUNKT
INNOVISION

# 11
# SERVING ON
# A PROTEST
# COMMITTEE

# 11 SERVING ON A PROTEST COMMITTEE

This little section is addressed to those yachtsmen who have the chance to serve as a member of a protest committee. You might think that if you want to get better at racing, to spend an evening or even an hour serving on a protest committee would be a waste of time and of no interest. Such is rarely the case. Even if you have no desire to serve your fellow competitors or the sport in this way, you should do it to further your knowledge, because in almost every protest hearing, everyone learns something.

## Your responsibility

Don't turn down an invitation to serve on a protest committee on the grounds that your knowledge of the racing rules is wanting. No-one understands all the rules, not even the people who wrote them. The most important task of the protest committee is to find facts which are as close as possible to what actually happened, and the qualities required to do that successfully are to be a good judge of people, to have patience, sympathy, understanding, knowledge of the types of yachts involved, a logical mind, and so on. Everyone has at least some of these qualities and, therefore, anyone can contribute something to a protest hearing. Your responsibility as a member is to be at the right place at the right time, having consumed no alcohol, be dressed in appropriate attire, and, if time allows, be showered and rested. Then listen carefully to the evidence, asking questions if you need further information, so that you are as sure as you can be about the relevant things that happened regarding validity and the incident itself. Finally, to apply the racing rules as they are, rather than how you think they should be.

## Chairing the committee

To be a good protest committee chairman you do need to have had at least some protest committee experience. The best experience is to serve on protest committees under chairmen who have earned your respect.

If you are new to chairing protest committees I highly recommend you have a rule book in front of you open at Appendix C1 - Protest Committee Procedure, and simply follow each step. You need not hide the fact that you are following the procedure in the rule book, as competitors will respect you for doing so. I must have chaired hundreds of protest committees, yet not infrequently I forget procedural items, often to my embarrassment.

When all the evidence has been given and you have dismissed the parties, invite each member to contribute his or her view. Allow a member holding a minority view about a relevant point a chance to convince the others.

## 'Beyond all reasonable doubt'

'Balance of probability' and 'Beyond all reasonable doubt' are two oft-used phrases in the law courts, and although the yacht racing hearing system is not a court of law, the two phrases do have some relevance.

When faced with conflicting evidence (which happens at just about every protest hearing!) and the two stories seem to be equally likely, an inexperienced protest committee may think it has an impossible task.

However, the committee doesn't have to put equal weight on the various bits of evidence. If they feel a witness seems to know what he's talking about, and seems honest, the committee members can put more weight on his evidence. Use the 'balance of probability' principal.

Only in the case of a 'rule 75 hearing' (addressing a gross breach of good sportsmanship or manners) will the test 'beyond all reasonable doubt' be applied. However, that doesn't mean that there must be 'no doubt'.

## Judging as a vocation

If you enjoy serving on protest committees, and you are not already a qualified judge, you might want to consider yacht race judging as a adjunct to racing, or even as an alternative pastime. Most major yachting nations have 'judging schemes' which bring together those interested in this branch of the sport, and award the title of 'National Judge' to suitably qualified and experienced sailors. The International Yacht Racing Union appoint International Judges who serve on international juries and publish a Judging Manual which describes standard procedures, the Case Book which contains useful cases submitted by national authorities and accepted as correctly decided by the IYRU Racing Rules Committee, and of course the Racing Rules themselves.

# FURTHER READING

Write or phone Fernhurst Books for a free colour brochure.

Fernhurst Books, Duke's Path, High Street, Arundel, West Sussex BN18 9AJ, Tel 01903 882277

We particularly recommend the following.

**The Rules in Practice** by Bryan Willis. Explains the current racing rules. Each common situation is shown in a photograph and the author explains what each boat may, must or must not do. Also contains parts I, IV and V of the current rules for reference.

**Tactics** by Rodney Pattisson. A gold medallist explains how to out-manoeuvre the rest of the fleet at the start and on each leg of the course. Also includes Match Racing and Team Racing.

**Mental & Physical Fitness for Sailing** by Alan Beggs, John Derbyshire & John Whitmore. An Olympic coach and psychologist explain how to get fit for sailing and how to tune your mind for competition.

**Wind Strategy** by David Houghton. Explains how to predict the wind on the racecourse. Gives examples of wind planning at a number of regatta venues, plus summary charts to laminate and take afloat.

**Sailpower** by Lawrie Smith & Andrew Preece. Explains the theory of sails, hulls, rigs and foils to the non-technically minded, and shows how to use the theory to sail faster.

**Knots & Splices** by Jeff Toghill. How to tie knots that stay tied and make splices you can trust. Each one is illustrated with a photo sequence.

**Sails** by John Heyes. Sails are the driving force behind any boat, so it is important to get them right. This expanded edition now covers yacht and dinghy sails, and includes a useful 'faultfinder' chapter.

**Helming to Win** by Ian Pinnell & Lawrie Smith. Two former Yachtsmen of the Year explain how to steer a boat to win in all wind strengths, sea states and on all legs of the course.

**Crewing to Win** by Andy Hemmings. The crew of a racing boat is as important as the helmsman. This is the only book to cover every aspect of crewing from club level to planning an Olympic campaign.

**Tuning your Dinghy** by Lawrie Smith. Here is a logical, systematic approach to the problem of setting up your boat and fine-tuning it for maximum speed on all points of sailing. Includes a trouble-shooting section.